2/4    " Bungle in the Jingle"    Michael Loftus 11/93

# Career Recovery

Best Practices in the
Vocational Rehabilitation of
Persons with Serious Mental Illness

Michael S. Shafer, Anne Middaugh,
Marshall Rubin, and Rosemarie Jones

The Community Rehabilitation Division
Department of Family and Community Medicine
The University of Arizona Health Sciences Center

TRN

Training Resource Network, Inc. ❖ St. Augustine, Florida

# Acknowledgments

The development of this material was supported in part by the Arizona Department of Economic Security, Rehabilitation Services Administration (Contract # E5345136), the U.S. Department of Education, Rehabilitation Services Administration (Grant #H128L20077), and The University of Arizona Health Sciences Center, Department of Family and Community Medicine. The opinions expressed in this handbook are strictly those of the authors and no official endorsement of the funding agencies is to be implied. The authors gratefully acknowledge the valuable contributions of Cyd Philippou, Sherry Hoskinson, Paula Koeck, Amelia Bryson, and the infinite patience of their families in the development and production of this book. Finally, the authors acknowledge the excellent feedback provided by Rick Baron and the Arizona RSA-BHS Interagency Services Committee members on an earlier draft.

# About the Authors

This book was developed collaboratively by four well-qualified professionals: Michael S. Shafer, Ph.D., Anne Middaugh, Ph.D., Marshall Rubin, A.C.S.W., C.I.S.W., and Rosemarie Jones. All of these individuals are experts in the fields of vocational rehabilitation, psychosocial rehabilitation, and community supports for persons with mental illness. Dr. Shafer received his degree in Urban Services from the Virginia Commonwealth University in 1988. Dr. Middaugh received her degree in Clinical Psychology in 1990 from George Washington University. Mr. Rubin received his M.S.W. from Rutgers University in 1964 and has over 28 years of experience in developing and administering rehabilitative community services for persons with serious mental illness. Ms. Jones received her Bachelors Degree in Special Education and Rehabilitation from The University of Arizona in 1993. All of these individuals are regular contributors to the professional literature, have extensive experience in the development and delivery of training and technical assistance materials, and are called upon regularly to consult with state and local community mental health and community rehabilitation agencies.

*Text editing, design, and layout by Cyd Philippou, M.F.A.*
*Cover artwork: "Bungle in the Jungle" a woodcut created by Michael Loghry, a Tucson artist and student at The University of Arizona, with extensive experience in working with the Vocational Rehabilitation system in Arizona.*
*Cover design: Training Resource Network, Inc.*

First Edition

This publication is sold with the understanding that the publisher is not engaged in rendering legal, financial, medical, or other such services. If legal advice or other such expert assistance is required, a competent professional in the appropriate field should be sought. All brand and product names are trademarks or registered trademarks of their respective companies.

Printed in the United States of America by BookCrafters.

Published by Training Resource Network, Inc., PO Box 439, St. Augustine, FL 32085-0439.

**Library of Congress Cataloging-in-Publication Data**

Career recovery : best practices in the vocational rehabilitation of persons with serious mental illness / Michael S. Shafer ...
  [et al.] — 1st ed.
    p.     cm.
  Includes bibliographical references.
  ISBN 1-883302-24-2 (trade paperback)
  1. Mentally ill—Employment—United States. 2. Mentally ill—Rehabilitation—United States. I. Shafer, Michael S.
(Michael Stephen), 1958-
HV3006.A4C365  1998
362.2'04256'0973—dc21
                                                                 98-2512
                                                                   CIP

# FIONA MARTIN

# Table of Contents

# Chapter 1

# An Introduction to Vocational Rehabilitation for Persons with Serious Mental Illness

The purpose of this handbook is to assist in the delivery of vocational rehabilitative services by pointing to demonstrations and suggestions of *best practice*. "Best practice," by definition, is often elusive and frequently subjective. As we will discuss later in this handbook, effective services must first be defined within the cultural and local context in which they will be delivered. Particularly for culturally and geographically diverse regions, the delivery of best practices in the provision of vocational rehabilitative services must be driven by sound empirical research and appropriate to local and cultural norms. As numerous researchers have pointed out, adopting and integrating a multi-cultural perspective also requires adoption and integration of a pluralistic orientation which accepts the evolving and situational nature of best practice.

Aside from the cultural and local variables influencing best practices, we can identify a series of common themes or values that should direct the delivery of vocational rehabilitative services to this population. Our search for best practices has been far reaching, driven by an exhaustive review of published research, project reports, and other printed material. Utilizing the computer search capabilities of the University's library, we have conducted literature searches of professional journals, textbooks, implementation guides, and other materials published within the past ten years. Additionally, we contacted major psychiatric and rehabilitation research centers across the country to obtain access to their most current research findings and updates on research in progress.

Unfortunately, the availability of scientifically rigorous research for all aspects of vocational rehabilitation of persons with serious mental illness is not consistently available, or of consistent quality. It is sometimes necessary to infer or extrapolate from related fields as they apply to the unique needs of this population. To the maximum extent possible, the observations and recommendations presented in the pages and chapters to follow are based upon current and defensible research with the population we commonly refer to as "seriously," "long-term," "chronically" or "severely and persistently" mentally ill. In certain circumstances, research from a related discipline or service area (community mental health services) or with a different disability population (substance abusers, developmentally disabled) is used to fill gaps in our understanding of best practice when working with this population.

## Vocational Characteristics and Needs of Persons with Serious Mental Illness

### What is Serious Mental Illness?

The term "serious mental illness," frequently used in the state of Arizona, refers to a specific subgroup of individuals deemed eligible for publicly-funded behavioral health services provided under the auspices of the Arizona Department of Health Services, Division of Behavioral Health. In this context, a person is considered seriously mentally ill when:

...as a result of a mental disorder, exhibit emotional or behavioral functioning which is so impaired as to interfere substantially with their capacity to remain in the community without supportive treatment or services of a long-term or indefinite duration. For these people, mental disability is severe and persistent, resulting in long-term limitation of their functional capacities for primary activities of daily living such as interpersonal relations, homemaking, self-care, employment, and recreation.

*A.R.S. 36-550(3)*

While the state of Arizona chooses to utilize the term "serious mental illness," a variety of other terms have been used to describe similar groups of individuals experiencing a mental illness, including *chronic, severe and persistent,* and *long-term.* Another similar description of the population was developed by National Institutes of Mental Health (1980):

...encompass(ing) persons who suffer certain mental or emotional disorders (organic brain syndrome, schizophrenia, recurrent depressive and manic-depressive disorders, paranoid and other psychoses, plus other disorders that may become chronic). These are disorders that erode or prevent the development of functional capacities in relation to three or more of such primary aspects of daily life as personal hygiene and self-care, self-direction, interpersonal relationships, social transactions, learning, and recreations, and that erode or prevent the development of economic self-sufficiency. Most individuals so diagnosed have required institutional care of extended duration, including intermediate-term hospitalization (90 days to one year in a single year), long-term hospitalization

(one year or longer in the preceding five years), nursing home placement for a diagnosed mental condition or diagnosis of senility without psychosis. Some such individuals have required short-term hospitalization (less than 90 days), others have received treatment from a medical or mental health professional solely on an out-patient basis, or despite their needs, have received no treatment in the professional-care service system. Thus, included in the target population are persons who are or were formerly "residents" of institutions (public and private psychiatric hospitals or nursing homes) and persons who are at high risk of institutionalization because of persistent mental disability.

*U.S. Department of Health and Human Services, 1980; pp. 2-11.*

Both of these definitions share common and critical elements in defining serious mental illness. First, severe mental disorders have increasingly been shown to be the result of discrete neurotransmitter and other biochemical imbalances. Second, serious mental illness results in serious economic, interpersonal, and functional limitations and hardships for those so identified. Third, individuals identified as seriously mentally ill require comprehensive and complementary services including primary health care, psychological counseling and interventions, and rehabilitation services to establish and/or restore functional capacities. What these definitions do not point out is that serious mental illness is not a single disorder, but a cluster of different disorders that, due to their resistance to traditional treatment, the severity of their resulting symptoms, and/or their extended duration of acuity, are considered to be disabling. This is important to understand when providing effective rehabilitation services.

### What are the Vocational Needs of Persons with Serious Mental Illness?

Nearly 1.5 million Americans suffer from a long-term mental illness. Of the total population of persons with severe mental illness, 79 percent report one or more specific limitations in work, school, personal care, social functioning, concentrating, or coping with day-to-day stress attributed to their mental illness. Over half (62%) of all persons with serious mental illness are reported as currently unable to work or limited in their work because of their disabilities. Many of these individuals will probably have several life experiences in common.

These individuals often lead lives that have been shattered as many of their most fundamental hopes, dreams, and aspirations are denied, or at the very least compromised, by the devastating havoc wreacked upon their life by this disability. These individuals may find themselves stuck in the revolving-door system of publicly-supported mental health care, moving back and forth between "stability" and "crisis" in managing their illness. Recovering from their illness and engaging in the challenges and rewards of becoming productive, valued members of their communities will be, at the very least, compromised by a system that often seems uncoordinated, if not uncaring. In all likelihood, these individuals will find themselves chronically unemployed, or at least under-employed, moving from one dead-end job to another without the opportunity to engage in a career or to pursue the promises of capitalism, productivity, and self-determination that have become the hallmarks of this country.

The unemployment of people with serious mental illness is so pervasive that Anthony (Anthony et al, 1988) noted that a person discharged from a hospital stands a better chance of returning to the hospital than of returning to work. Commonly accepted figures indicate that unemployment among people with serious mental illness may be as high as 90% (Mulkern and Manderscheid, 1989). More recently, the National Institute on Disability and Rehabilitation Research (1992) observed in a recent consensus statement that:

There is broad national consensus that the rates of unemployment and under-employment among people with psychiatric disabilities are unacceptably high. Despite their strong desire to work, their functional competencies, and their educational qualifications, many of those who suffer from severe and persistent problems have no long-term attachment to the labor market. The impact of this chronic unemployment and under-employment is severe, leaving individuals adrift and the nation deprived of their productivity.

*NIDRR, 1992*

Data from public vocational rehabilitation programs indicate that individuals with psychiatric disabilities have the lowest employment outcomes of any other disability group served in state and/or federal programs (NIHR, 1979, Marshak, Bostick & Turton, 1990), as well as employment retention problems that impede successful vocational achievement (Anthony & Blanch, 1987, MacDonald-Wilson, Mancuso, Danley & Anthony, 1989). MacDonald-Wilson reviewed reports from Rehabilitation Services Administration for fiscal year 1985 and found that people with serious mental illness represent the second most common type of client served by the federal-state rehabilitation system — 18% of the total clientele (MacDonald-Wilson et al, 1991). Ironically, this group has significantly higher rates of ineligibility determinations and unsuccessful closures, and significantly lower rates of successful closures, than other rehabilitation population groups (Marshak, et al., 1990).

## Variables Affecting the Vocational Success of Persons with Serious Mental Illness

Anthony, in his various writings with colleagues at the Center for Psychiatric Rehabilitation at Boston University, has found variables that predict vocational success:
- prior work history
- ability to get along with others
- degree of flexibility in problem approach.

Anthony and Jansen (1984) reviewed factors predictive of vocational capacity and concluded that diagnostic category was not related to employment success. Since then, Fabian (1992) and several other researchers have found a relationship between diagnosis, especially schizophrenia, and employment retention. Trotter et al (1988) reported that 83% of their sample who did not achieve employment placement were unsuccessful due to reasons associated with their psychiatric illness. Wehman, et al. (1990) indicated that almost 41% of job terminations for people with severe mental illness were due to factors that might be associated with psychiatric functioning, and Hanley-Maxwell, et al. (1986), found that 37.1% of terminations from supported employment program were due to social reasons.

Jacobs, Wissusik, Collier, Stackman and Burkeman (1992) found that psychiatric diagnosis was strongly correlated to outcome in their job club study. Persons with psychotic disorders such as schizophrenia or bipolar disorder were less likely to obtain jobs than persons with other disorders. These researchers noted that their model required a great deal of self-motivation and self-direction (i.e. making and following up on appointments, making "cold" calls to employers, and attending interviews). It may be that the amotivational, negative symptoms of schizophrenia interacted in a negative way with the model, suggesting the need for accommodation of the amotivational symptoms of schizophrenia in any vocational model adopted. They also found that good job interviewing skills often outweighed other negative predictive factors such as poor employment history and were predictive of success.

Russert and Frey (1991) write that the nature of psychiatric illnesses presents complex vocational problems. Normal vocational development from adolescence to adulthood is often interrupted resulting in vocational immaturity characterized by

unrealistic expectations and goals, limited or non-existent vocational histories, poor work habits and limited skill development. They also write that symptoms may impact vocational functioning, especially when outward symptoms affect work performance and tenure. Less intrusive symptoms — susceptibility to anxiety, difficulty with concentration, problems with memory and concrete problem solving, passivity and low motivation — also require management strategies. Katz, et al. (1990) reported anecdotal experiences of the interference of the symptoms of psychiatric disorders in the process of vocational rehabilitation.

Bond, Dietzen and Miller (1993) did not find demographic or psychiatric history variables affecting vocational success. Variables associated with employment outcome measures were: years of education, receipt of SSI or SSDI, and diagnosis (schizophrenia versus other). Despite Anthony's findings to the opposite, vocational history variables generally did not predict employment outcomes in their study, although the total hours of job coach contact did. What is obvious from these findings is that vocational rehabilitation of individuals with serious mental illness is a complex process. Rather than single factors affecting employment, a variety of interacting variables is probably involved, possibly different with each individual. It may be that different models or approaches are necessary for different individuals, rather than trying to develop one vocational rehabilitation model that works for everyone.

## Contemporary Influences and Approaches to Vocational Rehabilitation for Persons with Serious Mental Illness

During the past twenty years, significant strides have been made in the development of rehabilitation options and outcomes for individuals experiencing long-term mental illness. Most fundamentally, the focus of intervention has shifted away from the segregated setting of hospitals and institutions into the community. With this shift has come an emphasis on psychiatric rehabilitation, integrating into the mental health treatment a focus upon functional interventions that assist individuals in engaging in day-to-day activities of living, working and playing in their communities

(Anthony, Cohen, & Farkas, 1990). This psychiatric rehabilitation approach is holistic and functional, recognizing that interventions which facilitate functional skill use and engagement in valued life roles, particularly employment and education, can and should occur coupled with clinical interventions of symptom management and psychotherapy (Harding, Strauss, Hafer, & Lieberman, 1987). Today exemplary programs of community-based case management (Hodge, 1989; Intagliata, 1982) and Assertive Community Treatment (Stein & Test, 1985) have demonstrated the efficacy of providing interventions and supports to persons with mental illness in community settings. Significant strides have also been made in the utilization of psychopharmacological interventions in the control and reduction of the symptoms of mental illness (Safferman, Lieberman, Kane, Szymanski, & Kinon, 1991). The effective utilization of Lithium, Clozaril and other relatively-new medications have resulted in what some clients have described as a "re-awakening" as individuals, no longer arrested by the symptoms of their illness, and once again able to resume their lives (Wallis & Willwerth, 1992).

In addition to the advances in clinical interventions just described, the field of rehabilitation has been shaped by a number of other forces. Legislation, including the Americans with Disabilities Act and the re-authorization of the Vocational Rehabilitation Act (PL. 102-596), provides enhanced opportunities for

employment access and safeguards for individuals with disabilities, including those with a serious mental illness. While the ADA ensures greater access to employment and other community-based opportunities and services through reasonable accommodations, there remains much to learn about its implications for individuals with psychiatric disabilities (Mancuso, 1993). Nonetheless, the ADA, in conjunction with the recent amendments to the Vocational Rehabilitation Act of 1992, offers significant implications for the future of rehabilitation services to persons with a mental illness. Modified eligibility criteria, a greater emphasis on consumer and family involvement in service planning and program oversight, along with a general relaxing of the definition of employment with regard to weekly hours of employment, all provide promise for greater access to a more functional approach to accessing employment opportunities for persons with serious mental illness.

## Guiding Principles of Best Practice for Vocational Rehabilitation for Persons with Serious Mental Illness

The definition of "best practice" in the provision of vocational rehabilitation services to persons with serious mental illness has been attempted by many researchers and "expert panels" (Tashjian, Hayward, Stoddard, & Kraus, 1989; National Institute on Disability and Rehabilitation Research, 1992; Harding, Strauss, Hafer, & Lieberman, 1987; Institute on Rehabilitation Issues, 1988). Collectively, the work of these researchers and prestigious experts provide us with a number of benchmarks for assessing the quality of vocational rehabilitation service provision in general, and in particular, for those individuals considered seriously mentally ill. The Vocational Rehabilitation Act Amendments of 1992 describe seven guiding principles for the federal-state rehabilitation system (U.S. Department of Education, 1993). These principles provide an excellent framework for the conceptualization of vocational rehabilitation services.

1. Individuals with disabilities, including individuals with the most severe disabilities, are generally presumed to be capable of engaging in gainful employment;

2. Individuals with disabilities must be provided with opportunities to obtain gainful employment in integrated settings;

3. Individuals must be active participants in their own rehabilitation programs, including making meaningful and informed choices about the selection of their vocational goals, objectives, and services;

4. Families and natural supports can play an important role in the success of an individual's vocational rehabilitation program;

5. Qualified rehabilitation personnel can facilitate the employment goals of the individual with a disability;

6. Individuals with disabilities and their advocates are to be full partners in the rehabilitation program and be involved in a meaningful manner in policy development and implementation; and,

7. Accountability measures are to facilitate and not impede the accomplishment of the goals and objectives

of the Title I program, particularly with respect to serving individuals with the most severe disabilities.

While the chapters to follow will provide detailed information regarding discrete rehabilitative practices we consider to represent "best practice," there are some systemic or program-level variables and practices that have been identified as "best practice" when working with individuals considered seriously mentally ill.

Community Centered. First and foremost, researchers have stressed that the location of rehabilitation services must be in and about local communities. This community-centered orientation emphasizes not only the physical location of the delivery of services, but also the purpose of the services. That is, a predominant goal of the rehabilitation program should be on enhancing the community presence, participation, and overall functioning of the individual being served. Some researchers, noting the traditional social skill deficits of the population, have emphasized the importance of promoting relationships and interdependence among and between individuals with mental illness and their non-disabled communities (family members, neighbors, coworkers, etc.) (Condeluci, 1991; Rubin, 1994; Truer & Rubin, 1993). In contrast, other researchers have emphasized the importance of the community, particularly the work setting, as a critical location for the delivery of rehabilitative services (Cook, Jonikas, & Solomon, 1992). Likewise, the Community Support Program model, developed by the National Institute on Mental Health (Stroul, 1986), places strong emphasis on the community as the centered of local rehabilitation and mental health service provision.

Normalization. A recent poll by Louis Harris and Associates (1991) graphically illustrates the extreme prejudice, stigma, and discrimination that individuals with serious mental illness face. Among major disability groupings and deviant social groups (substance abusers, convicted felons, etc.), mental illness consistently evokes the most negative reactions regarding social distance and comfort among the general population. As such, researchers have emphasized that services to this population must be designed to be as non-stigmatizing as possible. From the name and location of the agency, to its service delivery methods, to its staff-client relations,

community mental health and rehabilitation agencies must be well grounded in the principles of normalization and social role integration, as supported by Wolfensberger and others (Carling, 1993).

Person-Centered Service Planning. Consistent with the underlying tenets of the Individual Written Rehabilitation Plan (IWRP), particularly in light of the most recent amendments to the Vocational Rehabilitation Act, is an emphasis on individualized and individually-driven assessment and service planning. As rehabilitation professionals, we accept the individuality of each client *irrespective of diagnosis, treatment history, or other client characteristics*. Rather, a person-centered approach to service planning acknowledges and works within a framework that remains sensitive and responsive to the unique needs, interests, and abilities of the individual client.

Strengths Based Assessment. Traditional approaches to vocational evaluation and assessment have tended to emphasize vocational skill deficits and weaknesses, and have generally been shown to be of limited value in effective rehabilitation service planning. This trend is consistent with advances in vocational assessment methodologies for other client populations and stresses the importance of what has been referred to as a *capacity-oriented* or *strengths-based* approach (Kisthardt & Rapp, 1989). These approaches to rehabilitation assessment and planning align with the inherent skills, capacities, and abilities of the client *and his/her social network*, rather than the limitations, deficits, and inability of the individual in isolation. Building upon these identified capacities, rather than attempting to remediate or overcome deficits, has been identified as a more effective and efficient approach to rehabilitation (Anthony, 1992).

Minimal Staff-Client Hierarchy. Particularly evident within those programs which may be described as clubhouses and psychosocial rehabilitation agencies (see Chapter 9) is a purposeful "blurring" or minimization of the hierarchical structures that separate "clients" from "staff." This minimization should also be evident in other rehabilitative agencies that provide services to persons with mental illness. As emphasized in the VR Act Amendments of 1992, the rehabilitation client should be an actively engaged and empowered member of the treatment planning team. Their personal experiences, their own knowledge of their illness and its history, as well as their personal preferences, dreams, and desires must be accepted with equal validity to the professional observations, opinions, and recommendations of the other, credentialed members of the treatment team. Given the educational level and knowledge of many individuals who have experienced a mental illness, along with the growing consumer orientation within the rehabilitation field, mental health consumers are increasingly finding themselves in a variety of paid and unpaid capacities within community mental health and rehabilitation agencies. Recent evidence has also suggested that mental health consumers, working as employment specialists, case managers, and other "professional" roles can be as effective in the delivery of rehabilitative services, when compared to non-mental-health-consumer staff (Cook et al., 1992; Stoneking, Greenfield, Sundby & Boltz, 1991).

Ongoing, Flexible, and Responsive Support System Availability. Consistent with the acknowledgment of mental illness as a severe disability, addressing the vocational rehabilitation needs of this population requires a multi-disciplinary approach that provides an array of community-based supports which are available over extended periods of time, in a manner that remains flexible and responsive to the individual needs of the client.

Integrated, Interdisciplinary Service Coordination. Finally, the critical role of interagency collaboration, cooperation, and coordination has been repeatedly emphasized as a critical dimension to the success of vocational rehabilitation options for individuals with serious mental illness (Harding et al., 1987; Anthony et al., 1992; Rezniek & Baron, 1991; Russert & Frey, 1991). Such coordination must involve, at a minimum, rehabilitation services, mental health case management, primary health care, psychiatric care, housing/residential support (if needed), and coordination with federal or private insurance benefits. This coordination and collaboration can take a variety of forms and degrees of implementation, ranging from informal agreements among agencies to fully integrated multi-disciplinary treatment teams. The underlying premise that agencies and professionals, each representing distinct and often divergent theoretical orientations, must learn to cooperate, collaborate, and coordinate, is a message that has been repeatedly stressed as a critical dimension of best practice for this population.

# References

Andrews, H. Baker, J. Pitman, J., Mars, L., Streuning, E, & La Rocca, H. (1992). National trends in vocational rehabilitation: A comparison of individuals with physical disabilities and individuals with psychiatric disabilities. *Journal of Rehabilitation, 58(1)*, 7-16.

Anthony, W., & Blanch, A (1987). Supported employment for persons who are psychiatrically disabled: An historical and conceptual perspective. *Psychosocial Rehabilitation Journal, 11*, 5-23.

Anthony, W.A., & Jansen, M.A. (1984). Predicting the vocational capacity of the chronically mentally ill--research and policy implications. *American Psychologist, 39*, 537-544.

Anthony, W.A., Cohen, M.R.,& Danley, K.S. (1988). The psychiatric rehabilitation model as applied to vocational rehabilitation. In J.A. Ciardiello, M.D. Bell (eds.) *Vocational Rehabilitation of Persons with Prolonged Mental Illness.* (pp. 59-80). Baltimore: Johns Hopkins University Press.

Anthony, W. (1992). Editorial. *Innovations and Research, 1(4)*, 1.

Anthony, W., Cohen, M., & Farkas, M. (1990). *Psychiatric Rehabilitation.* Boston, MA: Center for Psychiatric Rehabilitation.

Anthony, W. (1991). Recovery from Mental Illness: The new vision of services researchers. *Innovations & Research, 1(1)*, 13-14.

Anthony, W. (1993). Recovery from Mental Illness: The guiding vision of the mental health service system in the 1990s. *Psychosocial Rehabilitation Journal, 16(4)*, 11-23.

Anthony, W.A., Cohen, M.R., & Danley, K.S. (1988). The psychiatric rehabilitation model as applied to vocational rehabilitation. In J.A. Ciardiello, M.D. Bell (eds.) *Vocational Rehabilitation of Persons with Prolonged Mental Illness.* (pp. 59-80). Baltimore: Johns Hopkins University Press.

Black, B.J., & Kase, H.M. (1986). Changes in programs over two decades. In B.J. Black (ed.), *Work as Therapy and Rehabilitation for the Mentally Ill*, (pp. 3-37). New York: Altro Health and Rehabilitative Services.

Bond, G., Dietzen, L, & Miller, L., (1993) *Accelerating Entry into Supported Employment for Persons with Severe Psychiatric Disabilities*, Unpublished Manuscript.

Bond, G. (1992). Vocational rehabilitation. *Handbook of Psychiatric Rehabilitation*, Chapter 11. 244-275

Carling, P. J. (1993) Reasonable accommodations in the workplace for individuals with psychiatric disabilities. *Consulting Psychology Journal*, Spring, 46-62.

Condeluci, A. (1991). *Interdependence: The Route to Community.* Orlando, FL: Paul M. Deutsch Press.

Consensus statement (1992). Strategies to secure and maintain employment for people with long-term mental illness. *National Institute on Disability Rehabilitation Research, 1(3)*.

Cook, J.A., Jonikas, J.A., & Solomon, M.L. (1992). Models of vocational rehabilitation for youths and adults with severe mental illness: *American Rehabilitation, 6*.

Deegan, P. (1988). Recovery: The lived experience of rehabilitation. *Psychosocial Rehabilitation Journal, 11(4)*, 11-19.

Deegan, P.E. (1990). "How Recovery Begins." Presentation at the eighth annual Education Conference of the Alliance for the Mentally Ill of New York State.

Dincin, J. (1975). Psychiatric rehabilitation (Reprinted). *Schizophrenia Bulletin, 13*: 131-137.

Dincin, J., & Witheridge, T.F. (1982). Psychiatric rehabilitation as a deterrent to recidivism. *Hospital & Community Psychiatry, 33(8)*, 148-150.

Donaldson, T., Thomas, G., & Joiner, J.G. (1993). Issues in the vocational rehabilitation of persons with serious and persistent mental illness: A national survey of counselor insights. *Psychosocial Rehabilitation Journal, 16(4)*, 131-132.

Fabian, E. (1992). Longitudinal outcomes in supported employment: A survival analysis. *Rehabilitation Psychology, 37(1)*, 23-32.

Hagen, D.Q. (1983). The Relationship Between Job Loss and Physical and Mental Illness. *Hospital & Community Psychiatry, 34(5)*, 438-439.

Hanley-Maxwell., Rusch, F., Chadsey-Rusch, J., & Renzaglia, A. (1986). Reported factors contributing to the job terminations of individuals with severe disabilities. *Journal of the Association for Persons with Severe Handicaps, 11(1)*, 45-52.

Harding, C., Strauss, J., Hafer, H.& Lieberman, P. (1987). Work and mental illness. *The Journal of Nervous and Mental Disease, 175(6)*, 317-325.

Hodge, M. (1989). Supervising case managers. *Psychosocial Rehabilitation Journal, 12(4)*, 51-59.

Institute on Rehabilitation Issues (1988). *Enhancing the Rehabilitation of Persons with Long-Term Mental Illness.* Arkansas Research & Training Center in Vocational Rehabilitation. University of Arkansas, Fayetteville.

Intagliata, J. (1982). Improving the quality of care for the chronically mentally disabled: The role of case management. *Schizophrenia Bulletin, 8*: 655-674.

Jacobs, H., Wissusik, D., Collier, R., Stackman, D., Burkeman, D. (1992). Correlations between psychiatric disabilities and vocational outcomes. *Hospital and Community Psychiatry, 43:* 365-369.

Katz, L., Geckle, M., Goldstein, G., & Eichenmuller, A., (1990) A survey of perceptions and practice: Interagency collaboration and rehabilitation of persons with long-term mental illness. *Rehabilitation Counseling Bulletin, 33(4)*, 290-300.

Katz, L. (1991). Interagency collaboration in the rehabilitation of persons with psychiatric disabilities. *Journal of Vocational Rehabilitation, 1(3)*; 45-57.

Kisthardt, W., & Rapp, C. (1989). *Bridging the gap between principles and practice: Implementing a strengths perspective in case management.* Lawrence, KS: University of Kansas School of Social Welfare.

Louis Harris & Associates (1991). Public attitudes toward people with disabilities. Study No. 919028, conducted for the National Organization on Disability. New York, NY.

MacDonald-Wilson, K., Revell, W.G., Nguyen N.,& Peterson, M. (1991). Supported employment outcomes for people with psychiatric disability: A comparative analysis. *Journal of Vocational Rehabilitation, 1(3)*, 30-44.

Mancuso, L. (1993). Case studies on reasonable accommodations for workers with psychiatric disabilities. Community Support Program, Center for Mental Health Services and The California Department of Mental Health/California Department of Rehabilitation.

Marshak, L.E., Bostick, D.& Turton, L.J. (1990). Closure outcomes for clients with psychiatric disabilities served by the vocational rehabilitation system. *Rehabilitation Counseling Bulletin, 33*: 247-250.

Mulkern, V.M., Mandersheid, R.W. (1989). Characteristics of community support program

clients in 1980 and 1984. *Hospital and Community Psychiatry, 40:* 165-172.

National Institute on Disability and Rehabilitation Research. (1992). *Strategies to secure and maintain employment for people with long-term mental illness: Consensus statement.* Washington, DC: Author.

National Institute of Handicapped Research, Office of Special Education and Rehabilitation Services, US Department of Education (1979). *Past employment services and mentally disabled clients.* (Rehab Brief), Washington, DC: Author.

Reznicek, I., & Baron, R.C. (1991). *An Assessment of vocational rehabilitation/mental health collaboration on behalf of persons with long-term mental illness.* Philadelphia: Matrix Research Institute.

Rogers, E.S., Anthony, W.A., Toole, J., & Brown, M.A. (1991). Vocational outcomes following psychosocial rehabilitation: A longitudinal study of three programs. *Journal of Vocational Rehabilitation, 1(3)*: 21-29.

Rubin, M. (1994). Andrew and fellowship: Response to disaster in a psychosocial rehabilitation program: A hurricane tolerance test of structure, philosophy, and methodology. *An Introduction to Psychiatric Rehabilitation,* IAPSRS, 281-193.

Russert, M.G., & Frey, J.L. (1991). The PACT vocational model: A step into the future. *Psychosocial Rehabilitation Journal 14(4)*: 7-18.

Safferman, A., Lieberman, J., Kane, J., Szymanski, S. & Kinon, B. (1991). Update on the clinical efficacy and side effects of Clozapine. *Schizophrenia Bulletin, 1(3)*: 3-11.

Stein, L.I., & Test, M.A. (1985). The training in community living model: A decade of experience. *New Directions for Mental Health Services, 26.* San Francisco: Jossey-Bass.

Stoneking, B. (1992). *Consumers as an alternative labor pool.* The Center for

Community Change through Housing and
Support, Trinity College of Vermont.

Stoneking, B.C., Greenfield, T., Sundby, E., &
Boltz, S. (1991). *Adding trained consumers to
case management teams as service coordinators:
Program development, research design,
accommodations, and early outcomes.* Paper
presented at the 119th Annual Meeting of the
American Public Health Association, Atlanta,
Georgia, November 10-14.

Stroul, B.A. (1986). *Models of community
support services: Approaches to helping persons
with long-term mental illness.* Boston: Boston
University Center for Psychiatric Rehabilitation.

Tashjian, M. D., Hayward, B.J., Stoddard, S., &
Kraus, L. (1989). Best practice study of vocational
rehabilitation services to severely mentally ill
persons. *Policy Studies Associates, 1*: 15-21.

Trotter, S., Minkoff, K., Harrison, K, & Hoops, J
(1988). Supported work: An innovative approach
to the vocational rehabilitation of persons who are
psychiatrically disabled. *Rehabilitation
Psychology; 33*: 27-36.

Truer, E. & Rubin, M. (1993). *Direct Services
Guide*, Fellowship House, Miami, FL.

U.S. Department of Education (1993). *A Synopsis
of the Rehabilitation Act Amendments of 1992.*
Washington, DC: Rehabilitation Services
Administration.

U.S. Department of Health and Human Services,
(1980); pp. 2-11

Wallis, C., & Willwerth, J. (1992). Awakenings:
Schizophrenia: A new drug brings patients back
to life. *Time Magazine,* July 6, 53-60.

Wehman, P.W., Revell, W.G., Kregel, J.,
Kreutzer, J., Callahan, M., & Banks, D.B. (1990).
Supported employment: An alternative model for
vocational rehabilitation of persons with severe
neurological, psychiatric, or physical disabilities.
In J. Kregel, P. Wehman, M.S. Shafer (eds.),
*Supported employment for persons with severe
disabilities: From research to practice.*
Richmond: Virginia Commonwealth University.

# Chapter 2

# Strategies for Promoting Interagency Collaboration between Vocational Rehabilitation and Mental Health Agencies

The vocational rehabilitation of persons with serious mental illness requires interdisciplinary interventions and supports, provided in a flexible manner over an extended period of time. It is essential, then, that effective collaboration, coordination, and cooperation occur among and between individuals and agencies participating in an interdisciplinary treatment or support team. Effective interagency collaboration between federal, state, local, and private mental health and vocational rehabilitation agencies has long been identified to be crucial to the effective delivery of vocational rehabilitative services to this population. Similarly, the effectiveness of interagency efforts has been well documented in supported employment services (Hill et al., 1987), school to work transition (Halpern, Lindstrom, Benz & Nelson, 1991), and early intervention services (Elder & Magrab, 1980).

A recent study conducted in New York state is illustrative of the need for better interagency cooperation in providing vocational rehabilitation services to persons with serious mental illness. (Kaiser, Boothroyd & Evans, 1991). In this survey of community agencies providing supported employment, the lack of referrals of mental health consumers was identified as a major systemic barrier to the provision of services. State mental health officials noted that less than half of the community mental health programs in the state received funding from the state VR agency.

A lack of knowledge about VR funding mechanisms or awareness of VR as an agency that could fund employment services was identified as a major factor for this finding. Statewide, the researchers noted lack of linkages between programs as a major barrier to the provision of services.

The restrictions and requirements of community mental health agencies' other funding sources must also be acknowledged as a potential barrier to interagency collaboration with vocational rehabilitation. Most of these programs are heavily funded by state and federal Medicaid programs, under the funding authority of Title XIX of the Social Security Act. The funding restrictions of these programs and their negative impact upon the provision of vocational rehabilitation services has been well documented (Castellani, 1987; U.S. Department of Education, 1988). In particular, for persons with serious mental illness, program requirements and higher reimbursement rates for such services as partial hospitalization, day treatment, psychiatric counseling, and inpatient services (relative to those rates of psychosocial rehabilitation, behavior management, or VR services), may often serve as deterrents to VR referral. In order to fully appreciate the importance of interagency collaboration in providing vocational rehabilitation, it is helpful to review some of the traditions and theories of these separate areas of discipline, vocational rehabilitation and mental health service delivery.

# The Federal-State Rehabilitation System

## Underlying Philosophy of Vocational Rehabilitation

By definition, vocational rehabilitation is concerned with rehabilitating people for vocational activity. As defined by Jaques (1970), rehabilitation refers to a re-adaptation process following an injury or a disorder. Vocational rehabilitation has historically concerned itself only with those individuals who had acquired a disabling condition, either through an industrial mishap, an automobile accident, armed conflict, disease, or some other means. This early orientation shaped a rehabilitation philosophy that emphasized productivity and self-sufficiency. The orientation toward productivity and self-sufficiency is most pervasive in the eligibility requirements of the system. These requirements have historically mandated that applicants display the potential for full-time competitive employment and the potential that they could become self-sufficient and productive members of the labor force following rehabilitative services.

Public vocational rehabilitation can be characterized by three essential principles (Bitter, 1979). First, vocational rehabilitation supports equality of opportunity, particularly in the workplace. As such, vocational rehabilitation services to persons with disabilities are justified on the basis that these services will enhance individuals'' ability to experience the same opportunities for financial enrichment, career advancement, and self-enhancement that are available to able-bodied working individuals. Second, vocational rehabilitation assumes a holistic approach to treating clients. Services cannot be appropriately provided when they are not coordinated. Effective rehabilitation requires that the whole person be dealt with in a unified fashion that addresses all major facets of living. The third principle is an orientation toward individuality. In essence, this principle assumes that services are designed and provided to individuals on the basis of their unique and individual needs.

## The Rehabilitation Process

The rehabilitation process that most clients encounter consists of four basic steps: evaluation, planning, treatment, and termination (Rubin & Roessler, 1983). This process is an orderly and systematic sequence of activities that must be followed according to federal and state regulations. All clients applying to the system must first receive some form of evaluation before they can begin to receive services. This evaluation may be an informal process in which the counselor discussed vocational interests with the client. Conversely, such an evaluation may represent a formal referral to a vocational evaluation center where the client may be seen for a period of up to 18 months before actual services are initiated. Regardless of the formality or duration of this evaluation, all clients applying for services must receive some form of evaluation and all counselors must report that they provided some form of evaluation before actual services can be received.

One of the most comprehensive discussions of the sequential nature of the rehabilitation process was provided by Bitter (1979). Bitter's description is noteworthy because it discusses the rehabilitation process within the context of the case reporting system that is employed by the Rehabilitation Services Administration and each of the state vocational rehabilitation agencies. This system employs a series of status codes to represent various steps within the rehabilitation process as well as different services provided by the process. Status codes can be divided into four major types: referral processing (status codes 00 to 08), pre-service (status codes 10 to 12), in-service (status codes 14 to 24 and status code 32), and closure of active services (status code 26).

*Referral processing.* The referral process begins with a client applying for services from the state agency. Upon application, the client is assigned to a particular counselor who generally conducts an intake interview and attempts to make an initial determination that the client is eligible to receive vocational rehabilitation services. This determination is based upon the counselor's decision that the client exhibits a handicap that impedes employment potential and that the client can be reasonably expected to experience improved vocational potential as a result of receiving rehabilitation services. If the counselor is unable to make such a determination, the client may be referred for evaluation services for a period up to 18 months. When a counselor makes a determination that a client is not eligible to receive services, the client's case is terminated as an ineligible case closure (status 08). None of the activities conducted during this phase of the rehabilitation process are considered to be services to the client.

*Pre-Service.* This phase of the rehabilitation process begins once the client has been determined to be eligible to receive vocational rehabilitation services. Major activities that will occur during this phase of the process include the development of an Individualized Written Rehabilitation Plan (IWRP) and the arrangement of services to be provided to the client as identified by the IWRP.

Once the IWRP has been developed, the counselor may begin to arrange for the provision of services to the client. Typically, these services are provided by rehabilitation service providers other than the rehabilitation counselor. These providers may include a host of rehabilitation facilities such as work adjustment centers, vocational evaluation centers, sheltered workshops, and job placement agencies. Counselors generally will refer clients to these agencies and authorize the provision of a specified type, amount, or duration of service. These specifications are usually expressed in a unit service formula with the service provider receiving a fixed amount of revenue from the state agency for each unit of service.

*In-Service.* This phase of the rehabilitation process refers to the period during which clients actually receive vocational rehabilitation services that are designed to help them achieve their vocational objectives. Three basic types of services may be provided during this period: counseling, restoration, and vocational training. According to Bitter (1979), counseling (status 14) refers to counseling and guidance only and (possibly) placement services for preparing the client for employment. Restoration (status 16) include medical, surgical, psychiatric, or therapeutic treatment, and/or the fitting of a prosthetic appliance. Finally, training (status 18) refers to "any sort of learning situation, including school training, on-the-job training, work adjustment, tutoring, and training by correspondence" (Bitter, 1979. p. 38). These services are provided either individually or in combination until the client is considered ready for employment.

Once the client is considered ready for employment, placement into employment may be made. Once placement has been made, the client's status is considered to be in "trial employment" (status 22). The client must remain in this status for at least 60 days before case closure can occur. A final form of service that can be provided to clients is referred to as "post-employment." This refers to services provided to employed clients whose cases have already been closed, but who are in need of additional services to maintain their employment. Clients may receive these services without re-entering the rehabilitation system through the standard application and eligibility determination process.

Closure of active cases. Rehabilitation counselors may successfully "close" (status 26) the cases of clients who have maintained stable employment for 60 continuous days. Following case closure, the client is considered rehabilitated and the counselor will no longer provide or monitor services except in the unique situation of post-employment services that was previously discussed. In addition to status 26 closures, rehabilitation counselors may also terminate services to clients through two other closure codes. Status 30 closures refer to clients who were denied services and had their cases closed before the services were provided. These clients were either evaluated to be ineligible for services or had been evaluated as eligible and had an IWRP developed, but did not subsequently receive services. Status 28 closures represent clients who have received services but who failed to become successfully employed.

## Rehabilitation Counselors

Rehabilitation counselors represent a critical link in the rehabilitation process as they serve as the liaison between clients as the rehabilitation system. These individuals are responsible for monitoring, arranging and managing all facets of the rehabilitation process. Due to their global functions within the rehabilitation process, rehabilitation counselors have been characterized by some as the most important staff member in the rehabilitation process (Wright, 1980).

The specific functions that these counselors will perform is dependent upon the needs of the client, the nature and demands of the agency for whom they are employed, and the requirements of the community (Riggar, et al., 1986). However, a sample of activities that these counselors typically perform include: determining whether applicants are eligible and feasible, planning with clients the objectives and strategies for their rehabilitation, managing and arranging for necessary services, making client referrals to other agencies, providing ongoing counseling, keeping in contact with the client's family, and conducting or participating in job placement (Wright, 1980).

## The Federal-State Mental Health System

In sharp contrast to the consistency and uniformity that permeates the federal-state rehabilitation system, the provision of mental health services varies widely from state to state, and in some instances, county to county. This inconsistency is reflective of the lack of coordination and leadership that the federal government has provided in developing services for persons with mental illness. A rich legislative history exists regarding the development of mental health services, as in the case of Vocational Rehabilitation. In fact, the first major Federal Public Law affecting mental health services was passed as recently as in 1986.

In spite of the lack of Federal involvement, an underlying concept that has permeated behavioral health services during the past twenty years has been the Community Support Program (Stroul, 1986). This model provides a conceptual framework for developing comprehensive and coordinated systems of care for helping to support persons with mental illness. As noted by Brown and Basel (1988), the Community Support System was defined by the National Institute of Mental Health as "a network of caring and responsible people committed to assisting a vulnerable population to meet their needs and develop their potential without being unnecessarily isolated or excluded from the community" (pp. 26). These systems are designed primarily to maintain individuals in the community and out of costly and stigmatizing inpatient treatment facilities, including private and state psychiatric hospitals. Stroul (1986) identifies ten essential components that are needed to provide adequate opportunities and services for persons with serious mental illness. These include:

- Outreach to and Identification of Clients
- Assistance in Meeting Basic Human Needs
- Mental Health Care
- 24-Hour Crisis Assistance
- Psychosocial and Vocational Services
- Rehabilitative and Supportive Housing
- Assistance/Consultation and Education
- Recognition of Central Support Systems
- Grievance Procedures/Protection of Client Rights
- Case Management

Typically, individuals with serious mental illness are assisted in accessing these services by a case manager. These individuals serve a variety of functions, including gatekeeper, service coordinator, advocate, and therapist, as they assist clients maintain community tenure. In contrast to VR counselors who work within a well-established program with identifiable parameters, definable timelines, and explicit outcomes, mental health case managers will often find themselves engaged with clients over an extended period of time (years), involved in most facets of the client's life (not just employment), in which the specific outcomes of the relationship (either as imposed by the funding agency or stated by the consumer) has changed many times. In this regard, the roles of the case manager and the rehabilitation counselor will differ most significantly. While VR counselors are involved with clients in supporting career and employment objectives, mental health case managers may be involved with clients throughout most of the client's life.

## Federal Efforts at Interagency Collaboration

On the national level, the two federal agencies responsible for research and training on community treatment and rehabilitation of persons with serious mental illness are the National Institute of Mental Health (NIMH) and the National Institute on Disability and Rehabilitation Research (NIDRR). These agencies have conducted a number of interagency initiatives, including collaboration in the funding and oversight of the three Rehabilitation Research and Training Centers exclusively focused on the rehabilitation of persons with psychiatric disabilities. These Centers are currently located at the Thresholds Research and Training Center in Chicago, Illinois, the Matrix Research and Training Center in Philadelphia, Pennsylvania, and the Center for Psychiatric Rehabilitation at Boston University in Boston, Massachusetts. Additionally, the Rehabilitation Act Amendments of 1992 provide clear directives for interagency collaboration between state rehabilitation agencies and other state and local agencies. Specifically, these amendments call for:

- interagency collaboration between VR programs and other programs and agencies providing services to individuals with disabilities;

- training of staff of other programs regarding the availability and benefits of vocational rehabilitation services, and the provisions related to eligibility for services to enhance the access of individuals to such services; and

- cooperation among agencies through interagency working groups and formal interagency agreements.

*Department of Education (1993)*

## Benefits of Interagency Collaboration

The benefits of interagency collaboration between mental health, vocational rehabilitation and other agencies have been frequently addressed in professional literature (Dellario, 1985; Rezniek & Baron, 1991; Rogers, Anthony & Danley, 1990). While some of these studies may lack the level of methodological rigor to suggest causative relationships, these studies and others in related areas of research (transition, early intervention) have identified the following advantages to interagency collaboration:

1. Increased rates of acceptance for applicants to VR services
2. Increased rates of successful closure for VR services
3. Improved employment outcomes

4. Development of more appropriate services, as judged by case managers and rehabilitation counselors
5. Minimized conflicts between and among agencies, clients, and providers
6. Expanded relations with smaller agencies
7. Reduced duplication and overlap
8. Reduced gaps in the service system
9. Reduced waiting lists

Few detriments have been reported as resulting from interagency collaboration. In a survey of state VR and MH administrators, Rezniek and Baron (1991) reported an increase in the cost of service provision to clients who are jointly served by VR and MH agencies.

## Staff Training Needs of Interagency Collaboration

As specified by the Rehabilitation Act Amendments of 1992, training of staff on cross-agency access and service coordination is essential to effective interagency collaboration. In a recent survey of over 600 mental health and vocational rehabilitation staff, the lack of personal knowledge and skills about psychiatric illnesses was the most commonly identified area of skill deficit (Katz et al., 1990). The survey also identified knowledge about terminology, diagnostic skills, and treatment skills as areas in which staff lack competence. Knowledge of mental illnesses, including

symptoms, its cyclic nature, re-hospitalizations, and impact upon functioning was identified as the most needed skill for these professionals. The following table describes competencies that may be lacking in both VR and MH agency professionals:

|  | ...may lack knowledge of these terms: | ...may lack competence in these skills: |
| --- | --- | --- |
| Rehabilitation Professionals.. | • capitation<br>• ALFA<br>• co-pay<br>• clubhouse<br>• risk contracting<br>• partial care | • understanding psychotropic medications and their side effects<br>• de-escalation strategies and crisis referral<br>• a basic understanding of major DSM IV classifications and symptom classification |
| Mental Health Professionals.. | • "26"<br>• VALPAR<br>• time-limited<br>• TJTC<br>• reasonable accommodation<br>  trial work period | • submitting and managing work incentives<br>• assisting consumers to access post-secondary education<br>• helping consumers conduct job searches<br>• negotiating with employers |

## Strategies That Promote Interagency Collaboration

A variety of strategies have been identified that may promote or facilitate interagency collaboration (Dellario, 1985; Rezniek & Baron, 1991; Rogers et al., 1990). The following provides a partial listing of some of these strategies:

• Promoting Interpersonal Relationships. Dellario (1985), in a study of MH-VR interagency effectiveness in Oregon, observed that the quality of the interpersonal relationships between agency (VR and MH) staff is as critical as some of the more overt "systems-level" strategies that we will discuss in a moment. Interagency collaboration is most effective when rehabilitation counselors, case managers, and other professionals share a mutual respect for one another and a common purpose. It appears that developing a common understanding and respect of each professions' orientation, values, and "traditions" are important in the development of a meaningful interagency relationship. In describing interagency collaboration for preschool early intervention programs, Elder & Magrab (1980) note the importance of interpersonal relationships:

In its most meaningful sense, interdisciplinary (care) is an attitude. For professionals to interact in a truly collaborative manner, the elements of trust, respect, and mutual dependence must be present. In order to develop a decision-making and planning process that is interdisciplinary in nature, the professionals involved must recognize each other's competencies, trust each other's opinions, and rely upon each other...

*(pp. 17)*

• Creating Flexibility in the Interpretation and Enforcement of Agency Policies and Procedures. Flexibility around agency rules, regulations, and traditions has been identified as another important strategy to effective interagency collaboration (Harding et al., 1987; Rezniek & Baron, 1991). This flexibility represents a bi-lateral process where agencies *share* a great deal of flexibility concerning many of their own "sacred cows." Some of these include:
  • intake and eligibility criteria
  • case closure and treatment completion decisions and processes

- funding responsibility and authority
- duration of services
- referral criteria
- re-opening of cases
- authorized services

- Establishing Interagency Agreements. The development and implementation of both formal and informal agreements between various agencies is an effective means of ensuring interagency collaboration. For persons with serious mental illness, a comprehensive array of state and local agencies should include:
  - vocational rehabilitation
  - mental health
  - primary health care
  - state Medicaid administering agency
  - housing
  - education
  - corrections
  - law enforcement
  - welfare/food stamps
  - social security

Additionally, a variety of local and community organizations, including community mental health centers, community rehabilitation agencies, and advocacy organizations such as NAMI chapters and consumer-run organizations can play an important role in effective interagency agreements.

Developing and implementing effective interagency agreements is a difficult task. Frequently, these agreements are difficult to translate into actual service delivery practices. McLaughlin (as cited by LincFact, 1989) found that interagency agreements were most successful when those responsible for planning and implementing the agreement had a plan, started small, proceeded with order and method, approached each step in a timely and persistent manner, and communicated. Wehman, Moon, Everson, & Barcus (1988) suggests 25 characteristics of effective interagency agreements:

1. Definition of terms
2. Process of eligibility determination
3. Procedures for referring clients
4. Staff allocation from differing agencies

5. Procedures for implementing the agreement
6. Plan for dissemination of the Agreement
7. Plan for conducting cross-agency inservice workshops to agency personnel regarding requirements and restrictions of the Agreement
8. Time overlapping/service coordination
9. Listing of specific services available (both purchase of services and direct services)
10. Procedures for developing new services or programs
11. Specific arrangements for cost-sharing
12. Procedures for data and information sharing
13. Release of information and confidentiality procedures
14. Attendance/participation at IWRP/ISP meetings
15. Timeline or calendar for implementation
16. Schedule for re-negotiation, modification, and termination of agreement
17. Clear delineation of client population covered by the agreement
18. Schedule of interactions/meetings between agencies
19. Mission statement/purpose of the Agreement
20. Desired outcomes of the Agreement
21. Procedures for disseminating information to consumers and family members regarding service availability
22. Procedures and schedule for conducting needs assessment and follow-up surveys of clients
23. Specific responsibilities of all signature agencies
24. Identification of agency liaisons
25. Policy statement(s) regarding service delivery

- Promoting Understanding and Respect for Interagency Differences. Understanding and respecting the theoretical bases of mental health and vocational rehabilitation is another strategy for enhancing interagency collaboration. Both agencies (VR and MH) have different orientations toward the provision of services to persons with mental illness. Mental health professionals are typically trained and operate within medically-oriented service models, often driven by the acuity of disorders. Vocational rehabilitation professionals follow a rehabilitative model in which the focus is on the restoration of functioning. Understanding this basic difference, and the implications for consumers and intervention strategies, is fundamental.

- <u>Collocating Mental Health and Vocational Rehabilitation Personnel</u>. Collocating mental health and vocational rehabilitation staff has also been demonstrated to be an effective strategy for promoting interagency collaboration. This model has been well described by the Assertive Community Treatment model of Stein and Test (1985) . The PACT vocational model (Russert & Frey, 1991) and the more recent description of the Individual Support Program (Becker & Drake, 1993) provide strong support for the value of

physically, and to some extent administratively, integrating mental health and vocational rehabilitation staff. The PACT model, representing an evolution of Stein and Test's (1985) archetypal work on Assertive Community Treatment (ACT), describes an integrated model of vocational service delivery wherein the mental health specialists and vocational rehabilitation specialists are administratively and physically housed within a single entity.

## Best Practice Indicators

Best practices in promoting interagency collaboration in the provision of vocational rehabilitation services to persons with serious mental illness include:

1. Developing systems that maximize access and information sharing between agencies. Examples include shared paperwork systems, common forms, and integrated/joint service planning processes.

2. Collocating vocational rehabilitation staff, including counselors, employment specialists, and job developers, within community-based and accessible locations.

3. Providing regular and frequent opportunities for cross-training between agencies and promote cross-agency relationship building.

4. Providing flexibility in the interpretation of agency policies and rules.

5. Ensuring consistent demonstrated support and involvement of interagency initiatives at all levels within the agencies, beginning with the top administrators.

## References

Becker, D., Drake, R, (1993) A Working Life: The Individual Placement and Support (IPS) Program. New Hampshire: Dartmouth Psychiatric Research Center.

Bitter, J.A. (1979). *Introduction to Rehabilitation*. St. Louis: C.V. Mosby.

Brown, M. & Basel, D. (1988). Understanding differences between mental health and vocational rehabilitation: A key to increased cooperation. *Psychosocial Rehabilitation Journal, 12*: 23-33.

Castellani, P. (1987). The Political Economy of Developmental Disabilities. Baltimore: Paul H. Brooks Publishing Co., Inc.

Dellario, D. J. (1985). The relationship between mental health, vocational rehabilitation interagency functioning and outcome of psychiatrically disabled persons. R*ehabilitation Counseling Bulletin, 28*(3) 167-170.

Elder, J. O., Magrab, P. R, (1980). Coordinating Services to Handicapped Children - A Handbook for Interagency Collaboration. Paul H. Brooks Publishing Company, Inc.

Goodwin, L. (1992). Rehabilitation counselor specialization: The promise and the challenge. Journal of Applied Rehabilitation Counseling, 23(2), 5-11.

Halpern, A., Lindstrom, L., Benz, M. & Nelson, D. (1991). *Community Transition Team Model*. University of Oregon.

Harding, C.M., Strauss, J.S., Hafez, H., Liberman, P.B. (1987).Work and Mental Illness. The Journal of Nervous and Mental Disease, 175, 318-325.

Hill, M. L., Revell, G., Chernish, W., Morell, J. E., White, J., Metzler, H., MaCarthy, P. (1987). Planning for Change: Interagency Initiatives for Supported Employment.

Jacques, M.E. (1970). *Rehabilitation Counseling: Scope and Services*. Boston: Houghton Mifflin.

Kaiser, P., Boothroyd, R., & Evans, M. (1991) *Special Employment Progarms: An Analysis of Staff and Client Characteristics, client Satisfaction and Outcomes*. Bureau of Evaluation and Services Research, New York Sate Office of Mental Health.

Katz, L.J., Geckle, M., Goldstein, G., & Eicenmuller, A. (1990). A survey of perceptions and practices: Interagency collaboration and rehabilitation of persons with long-term mental illness. *Rehabilitation Counseling Bulletin, 33*(4) 290-300.

McLaughlin, J. (1989). As cited in Lincfact, Missouri LINC, University of Missouri-Columbia, No.11.

Noble, J., Collignon, F. (1987). Systems barriers to supported employment for persons with chronic mental illness. Psychosocial Rehabilitation Journal, 11(2), 25-43.

Rezniek, I., Baron, R.C. (1991). An Assessment of vocational rehabilitation/mental health collaboration on behalf of persons with long-term mental illness. Philadelphia: Matrix Research Institute.

Rogers, E.S. Anthony, W.A., & Danley, K.S. (1990). The impact of interagency collaboration on system and client outcomes. *Rehabilitation Counseling Bulletin, 33* (2), 100-109.

Rogers, E.S., Anthony, W.A., Toole, J.& Brown, M.A. (1991). Vocational outcomes following psychosocial rehabilitation: a longitudinal study of three programs. *Journal of Vocational Rehabilitation, 1*(3), 21-29.

Rubin, S.E. & Roessler, R.T. (1983). *Foundations of the Vocational Rehabilitation Process*. Baltimore: University Park Press.

Russert, M.G., & Frey, J.L. (1991). The PACT vocational model: A step into the future. Psychosocial Rehabilitation Journal 14(4), 7-18.

Stein, L.I., Test, M.A. (1985). The Training in Community Living Model: A Decade of Experience. *New Directions for Mental Health Services, 26.* San Francisco: Jossey-Bass.

Stroul, B.A. (1986). *Models of community support services: Approaches to helping persons with long-term mental illness.* Boston: Boston University Center for Psychiatric Rehabilitation.

Tashjian, MD., Hayward, B.J., Stoddard, S., Kraus, L. (1989). Best Practice Study of Vocational Rehabilitation Services to Severely Mentally Ill Person: Policy Studies Associates, Vol. 1, p.15-21.

U.S. Department of Education (1988). *Summary of Existing Legislation Affecting Persons with Disabilities.* Washington, DC: Office of Special Education and Rehabilitation Services, Clearninghouse on the Handicapped.

U.S. Department of Education (1993). *A Synopsis of the Rehabilitation Act Amendments of 1992.* Washington, DC: Rehabilitation Services Administration.

Wehman, P., Moon, M. S., Everson, J. M., Wood, W., Barcus, J. M. (1988). Transition from School to Work. Paul H. Brooks Publishing Company, Inc.

Wehman, P., Moon, M. S., Everson, J. M., Wood, W., Barcus, J. M. (1988). Transition from School to Work. Paul H. Brooks Publishing Company, Inc.

Wehman, P., Moon, S. Everson, J., Wood, W., Barcus, M. (1985). Life Beyond the Classroom. Paul H. Brooks Publishing Company.

Wright, G.N. (1980). *Total Rehabilitation*. Boston: Little, Brown and Company (Inc.).

# Chapter 3

# Best Practices in Referral and Intake and Service Planning

Best practice for providing vocational rehabilitation services to persons with serious mental illness is maintained by a well coordinated, comprehensive array of community-based services. A comprehensive system requires a process of client referral, eligibility assessment, and service planning that maximizes utilization of existing resources and information, minimizes gaps and delays between agencies, and coordinates service planning within and between agencies. To date, little empirical information is available regarding the efficiency of different referral models or intake processes in achieving these aims. However, the 1992 Amendments to the Vocational Rehabilitation Act clarified a number of critical elements regarding the intake and service planning process for the federal-state vocational rehabilitation system. Most notably, these amendments altered eligibility criteria, quickened the pace at which eligibility decisions must be rendered, and expanded the requirements of the IWRP.

## The 1992 Amendments and Intake and Service Planning Procedures

Eligibility for services by vocational rehabilitation has traditionally included an assumption that some individuals, particularly those with severe handicaps including serious mental illness, were incapable of work and therefore should not be served by Vocational Rehabilitation. Under this model, the function of VR intake and referral processing was to identify and exclude those individuals deemed incapable of benefiting from VR services. The 1992 Amendments eliminated this assumption and unequivocally articulate a presumption that individuals with disabilities, irrespective of the severity, are able to benefit from VR services in terms of employment (Community Support Network News, Spring/Summer 1993; Virginia Commonwealth University, Winter 1993). Furthermore, these amendments place the burden of responsibility for establishing ineligibility on the state VR system by requiring rehabilitation counselors to provide *clear and convincing evidence* that an individual is incapable of benefiting from VR services. The use of such legalese was intentional and designed to stress the seriousness with which state VR agencies should approach the process of service denial.

The 1992 Amendments also required state VR agencies to speed up the time taken to process an application and determine eligibility for services. Long delays between applying for and receiving services has been a frequent complaint of the federal-state VR system. The 1992 Amendments require that applications are processed within 60 days, and eligibility determinations made within this time period. Extensions to this requirement can be provided, based on the mutual agreement of the applicant and the VR counselor.

## Best Practices in Referral Procedures

Best practice in referral to vocational rehabilitation services suggests a system that allows for multiple points of referral, ensures cross-agency information sharing, and coordinates complementary service provision among agencies. Interagency collaboration has a significant positive influence upon referrals to the

VR system. Tashjian, Hayward, Stoddard and Kraus (1989) reported that approximately half of all VR and mental health agency staff surveyed reported that they regularly attended meetings with staff from other agencies, primarily to review potential VR referrals. The same study found that formalized procedures for coordination between VR and mental health agencies streamlines consumer entry into the VR system, including using the referring agency's files on the applicant and regular, consistent communication. Problems regarding "inappropriate referrals" were diminished when VR and mental health collaborated to develop functional criteria for determining vocational readiness. Finally, the vocational rehabilitation staff surveyed in this study reported that collocation of VR counselors within mental health agencies was associated with increased appropriateness of referrals and decision making regarding mutual clients.

Becker and Drake (1993) recommend three characteristics of an effective referral process. First, the system should require a simple process of referral and minimize the amount of information necessary to initiate the referral (name, address, diagnosis, brief work history and current work goals). Second, they recommend providing good program information to all referral sources and potential clients to enhance the likelihood that informed individuals will enter the program with realistic expectations. Finally, they recommend a referral system that is open: self-referrals, case management referrals, and referrals from other agencies in the community. They warn against creating an agency "gatekeeper" for the program. Checks and balances to the referral system, in their model, are established within the integrated team approach. Becker and Drake (in press) add that an additional component of the referral decision is the individual's expression of interest in competitive employment. Their research indicates that a high proportion of those who select their vocational program themselves are able to obtain competitive jobs.

Effective VR referral practices should also include an active program of client outreach and recruitment. Aggressive outreach and client recruitment has long been identified as an important element of a comprehensive community support model (Russert & Frey, 1991; Stein & Test, 1985). Chamberlin, et al (1989), stresses the importance of outreach:

> Outreach is a word that captures the very essence of what excellent care is all about. Outreach demands that attention be paid to fashioning help based on who the person is and what her or his needs are. Client identification must consist of a name, a face, a body, a voice, a whole personality and, especially a life before and after mental illness. Outreach is not shuffling a mentally ill person from one agency to another, or telling a person or family in critical need to call back Monday morning. Outreach implies a seeking out of those who need help and a willingness to adapt services to the needs and circumstances of each individual.
> (p. 103)

Community mental health centers typically contain many potential referral sources. It is important for rehabilitation counselors to identify these referral sources and establish collaborative cross-agency outreach and referral initiatives. The referral sources a rehabilitation counselor should consider include:

- local family or consumer self-help organizations
- residential providers (group homes, board and care facilities, etc.)
- drop-in centers and clubhouses
- partial hospitalizations or day treatment programs
- psychiatric inpatient units
- local mental health case management agency

## Best Practice in Intake Procedures

Best practice for conducting intake to the VR process is the gathering of information that is directly related to the vocational goal — e.g., medication problems that might interfere with completing work tasks, access to transportation, and/or symptoms that may interfere with learning or memory of work task. Interviewing often forms the core of the vocational eligibility and planning process (Berven, 1984). However, clinical judgment, which is a common element in most unstructured and semi-structured interviewing approaches, has proven to be disappointing for predicting rehabilitation outcomes. Dawes, et al. (1989), has shown that clerks perform better by applying mechanical decision rules than trained clinicians when both are provided the same information. Practitioners often do not combine information very effectively; rather, they tend to form a small number of hypotheses early in the data-gathering process and their opinions then become resistant to change (Berven, 1984). Clinical interviewing instruments such as the Boston University Functional Assessment Approach (Farkas & Anthony, 1989), the VR Counselor Positive and Negative Indicators (Marrone, Horgan, Scripture, and Grossman, 1984) and the PACT Interview Guide (Rutkowski, 1990) should be used with caution and never as the sole determinant of readiness, functioning or placement.

The function of intake and assessment for vocational rehabilitation was changed fundamentally by recognition of the importance of informed choice in the vocational rehabilitation process. Intake and assessment have attempted to establish program eligibility by determining an individual's presumed vocational capacity. Questions typically asked in this paradigm included: "Can the person work?", "What are the person's skill deficits?", and "What is the person capable of doing?" Now, however, the intake and assessment process must also identify accommodations, support and resource needs, and most importantly, personal values and choices necessary to achieve employment. Questions to be asked under this paradigm include: "Do you want work?", "What are your support needs?", and "What resources (financial, interpersonal, environmental) do you have access to in order to achieve your rehabilitation goals?"

One approach to facilitating the intake process is the provision of work orientation classes or groups (Fabian & Wiedefeld, 1989; O'Brien, 1992). Fabian & Wiedefeld (1989) describe a seven-week intake group. The purpose of the weekly, two-hour group was to orient members to the supported employment model, to provide information about disability benefits and to begin defining work values and vocational choices. Issues such as grooming, entitlement, career choice, support, transportation and mental health were also addressed. Following participation in this group, individuals experienced accelerated placement into competitive employment. They noted that the relationship building that occurred during this intake phase was a significant factor in their successful placement. A recent study of VR clients with psychiatric disabilities revealed that nearly one-third of the cases of individuals with psychiatric disabilities were closed because they were unable to complete the IWRP discussion or the objectives set forth in the IWRP to which they had agreed (Marshak, Bostick & Turton, 1990). These results suggest that a more focused process of intake which emphasizes an orientation to the VR process and the development of a collaborative relationship with the rehabilitation counselor may increase the ability of individuals with serious mental illness to be successful in later stages of the VR process. As a result of such orientation groups, clients appear to be better informed to make choices about their rehabilitation goals and service plans. Unfortunately, little research has been conducted to date on the effectiveness of such orientation groups.

Efforts to minimize the delay between application and eligibility, and eligibility and service provision (and placement), appear to be critical for persons with serious mental illness. Best practice in determining the optimal time between application and service initiation may be different depending on the individual seeking services. Individuals with long job histories and more education may require a longer "choose" state (Wallace, 1993) than individuals who have no job histories. Bond (1987), however, notes that those individuals with prior work history especially benefit from rapid entry into community employment.

## Best Practice in Service Planning

One of the more significant changes in the 1992 Amendments had to do with modifications mandated for the Individual Written Rehabilitation Plan (IWRP).

Consistent with the consumer-driven values of the Act, the 1992 Amendments include a number of *"Choice Regulations"* in defining the IWRP. The IWRP must:

- be jointly developed between the individual and the counselor
- be designed to achieve the employment objectives of the individual
- be consistent with the individual's strengths, priorities, abilities and capabilities
- be designed to include a statement, in the individual's words, describing how he or she was informed of and involved in choice related to:
  1. employment goals
  2. objectives
  3. services
  4. service providers
  5. methods used to procure or provide services.
- be designed to include information regarding related services and benefits
- be provided in the language or mode of communication of the individual
- be agreed upon by the individual and the counselor
- be signed by the individual and the counselor
- be copied to ensure that the individual has his/her own copy of the final document
(*VCU Newsletter, Winter 1993*)

IWRPs that reflect best practice are specific and include goals and objectives that are concrete and measurable. The IWRP should specify:

- Which services will be provided at each stage of the rehabilitation process [Sec.101(a)(5)(C)(i)] and the ultimate outcome of goal of each service.
- A plan for establishing cooperative or interactive relationships with other agencies involved in the rehabilitation of the individual (i.e. vocational providers, case managers, psychiatrists).

The IWRP should be congruent with a functional assessment of an individual's strengths, priorities, abilities and capabilities. That is, all services identified as part of the IWRP, must be services that the individual is functionally able to access, use and will assist in achieving his/her objectives. If functional assessment identifies areas of deficits that would interfere with using identified services, the IWRP should specifically state plans for accommodating the needs to enable the person to benefit from the identified service, or should identify comparable services (that will achieve the objective) that the person is able to use.

Inclusion of individuals in the development of their IWRP involves many of the practical measures identified to involve individuals in the intake process. These include:

- flexibility in the length and location of planning sessions
- use of language that reflects the consumer and is easily understood by the consumer (avoid jargon)
- identifying and respecting the choices of the individual
- incorporating a focus on strengths and avoiding a focus on deficits

Individuals with serious mental illness are often very sensitive to body posture, tone of voice and language choice that conveys either a lack of respect or a lack of belief in rehabilitation potential. Attention to voice tone, posture and word choice can positively impact the planning relationship, avoiding power struggles and achieving an increased willingness to negotiate and compromise from the individual.

# Best Practices for Referral and Intake

A number of characteristics can be identified that, due to legal requirements, experimental validation, or consensus, can be considered "best practice" in providing intake and referral services for VR services to persons with serious mental illness.

- Multiple points of referral and intake within the system. Shared forms and information.
- Increased community outreach and education, both to consumers and to community agencies.
- Flexibility and the application of reasonable accommodations into the intake process.

- Focus on relationship building and the creation of a collaborative relationship during the intake process, rather than a focus on record keeping.
- Empirical research into referral and intake practices and their relationship to vocational program retention and employment retention.
- Intake process that orients the individual to vocational rehabilitation and clarifies expectations and needs.

- Intake process that includes an array of choices and options in the service delivery area; i.e. based on available services and providers.
- Checks and balances in the referral and intake process through an integrated team rather than a bureaucratic gatekeeper.

# References

Becker, D., Drake, R, (1993) *A Working Life: The Individual Placement and Support (IPS) Program.* New Hampshire: Dartmouth Psychiatric Research Center.

Becker, D., Drake, R (in press) Individual placement and support: A community mental health center approach to vocational rehailbiation. *Community Mental Health Journal.*

Berven, N. (1984). Assessment practices inr ehabilitation counseling. *Journal of Applied Rehaibitation Counseling,* 15: 9-14, 47.

Bilby, R. (1992) A response to the criticisms of transitional employment. *Psychosocial Rehabilitation Journal,* 16, 69-82.

Bond, G., & Dincin, J. (1986). Accelerating entry into transitional employment in a psychosocial rehabilitation agency. *Rehabilitation Psychology,* 31, 143-155

Bond, G. (1987) Supported work as a modification of the transitional employment model for clients with psychiatric disabilities. *Psychosocial Rehabilitation Journal,* 11: 55-73.

Bond, G., Dietzen, L, & Miller, L., (1993) *Accelerating Entry into Supported Employment for Persons with Severe Psychiatric Disabilities.* Unpublished Manuscript.

Chamberlin, J., Rogers, J.A., & Sneed, C.S., (1989). Consumers, Families, and Community Support Systems, *Psychosocial Rehabilitation Journal,* 12(3); 93-106.

Dawes, R., Faust, D., Meehl, P. (1989). Clinical versus actuarial judgment. *Science,* 243: 1668-1674.

Fabian, E, Wiedefeld, M (1989), Supported employment for severely psychiatrically disabled persons: A descriptive study. *Psychosocial Rehabilitation Journal,* 13: 53-60.

Farkas, M. & Anthony, W. (1989). *Psychiatric rehabilitation programs: Putting theory into practice.* Baltimore, MD: Johns Hopkins University Press.

Fraser, V. (1987). Adapting a psychosocial rehabilitation agency to a rural community. Psychosocial Rehabilitation Journal, 11(4), 67-71.

Russert, M.G., & Frey, J.L. (1991). The PACT vocational model: A step into the future. *Psychosocial Rehabilitation Journal 14(4):* 7-18.

Jones, G.I., (1986). Social adjustment, vocational and employment services for the chronically mentally ill: A system-integrated model. Psychosocial Rehabilitation Journal, 10(2), 46-54.

Kaiser, P., Boothroyd, R., Evans, M. (1991) Special Employment Programs: An analysis of staff and client characteristics, client satisfaction and outcomes. Bureau of Evaluation and Services Research New York Sate Office of Mental Health.

Marshak, L, Bostick, D, Turton, L (1990). Closure outcomes for clients with psychiatric disabilities served by the vocational rehabilitation system. *Rehabilitation counseling Bulletin, 33:* 247-250.

Marrone, J., Horgan, J., Scripture, D. & Grossman, M. (1984). Serving the severely psychiatrically disabled client within the vocational rehabilitation system. *Psychosocial Rehabilitation Journal, 5(2);* 5-23.

McKenna, Maureen (1993). Using Behavioral Rating Scales as Part of Vocational Assessment. *Sixth Annual Conference on Vocational Assessment.* Wisconsin-Stout

Mosher, L., Burti, L (1992). Relationships in rehabilitation: when technology fails. *Psychosocial Rehabilitation Journal, 15:* 11-17.

Noble, J. & Collignon, F. (1987). Systems barriers to supported employment for persons with chronic mental illness. *Psychosocial Rehabilitation Journal, 11*: 25-44.

O'Brien, W. F. (1993). *Psychiatric Rehabilitation Approach: Assisting Individuals with Severe Psychiatric Disabilities into Integrated Employment Opportunities.*

Rutkowski (1990). *Integrating community support programs and vocational rehabilitation.* Presentation at 1990 Speakers Series on Supported Employment and Psychiatric Rehabilitation. Department of Psychology (UPU), Indianapolis, IN.

Tashjian, M. Hayward, B Stoddard, S., Kraus, L. (1989). Best practice study of vocational rehabilitation services to severely mentally ill persons. *Vol I: Study Findings.* Policy Studies Associates, Inc. Washington, D.C.

Trotter, S., Minkoff, K., Harrison, K, Hoops, J (1988). Supported work: An innovative approach to the vocational rehabilitation of persons who are psychiatrically disabled. *Rehabilitation Psychology, 33*: 27-36.

Wallace, C. (1993). Psychiatric Rehabilitation. *Psychopharmacology Bulletin, 29*: 537-548.

*Community Support Network News* (1993). Boston: Boston University Center for Psychiatric Rehabilitation. Spring/Summer.

Virginia Commonwealth University (1993). *PL 102-569: The Rehabilitation Act Amendments of 1992.* Winter.

# Chapter 4

# Best Practice in Vocational Assessment and Evaluation

Best practice in vocational assessment has undergone a great deal of change over the past 50 years. Central to these changes is the need for balance between the experience and viewpoints of rehabilitation professionals and the consumer's activism and choice. To facilitate assessment that works, we must arrive at a common framework and vision for the practice and outcomes of vocational assessment (Urofsky, 1993).

Vocational rehabilitation counselors have several goals when they conduct, purchase or contract for vocational assessments. They need to know that the assessment was necessary, that the assessment will answer questions relevant to employment support planning, that the cost of the assessment can be justified, and that the assessment will justify the cost of contracted services. Furthermore, they need assessments that create workable and achievable IWRPs and present results and recommendations that are understandable to themselves, their providers and their customers. Vocational assessment has been defined as a process of assisting the job seeker in making career decisions and developing a plan of action to enter the job market (McDaniel & McClanahan, 1993).

Tashjan, et al., (1989), reports the results of a national poll of rehabilitation counselors in which the following vocational assessment procedures were identified to be most effective:
- situational assessment
- general vocational evaluation
- psychiatric evaluation
- personal interviews

Corroborating data are presented by Hursh, Rogers and Anthony (1988) who interviewed 418 rehabilitation professionals working primarily with individuals with psychiatric disabilities. These researchers reported that the major reason identified for conducting or requesting a vocational assessment was to assess clients' skill ability. Other reasons included opportunity for vocational exposure and the identification of feasible vocational alternatives. Situational assessment was the preferred method of assessment by 48% of the respondents. Diagnostic interviewing and work sample evaluations were preferred by significantly fewer of the respondents ( 20.7% and 16.2% of the respondents, respectively).

The reliability and validity of vocational assessments can be affected by many variables, especially: the impact of aids, adaptation and helpers; the environment in which the assessment takes place; motivational factors; the professional's perspective; and the individual's perspective (Kaufert, 1983). To counteract these effects, vocational assessments should utilize an array of methodologies and draw upon information derived from a variety sources, including the client, family members, peers and coworkers, and other significant individuals. Dellario, Goldfield, Farkas & Cohen (1984) identified five characteristics or competencies of the individuals conducting vocational assessments that enhance the reliability and accuracy of information derived by these processes:

1. An attitude emphasizing capacities specific to environmental demands independent of symptoms or functioning in other environments
2. Knowledge about environments
3. Skills to involve consumers in the evaluation process
4. Skills to identify concrete behaviors as performed in a specific environment

5. Skills to assess the amount of current behavior and the amount of behavior required in the environment.

In this chapter, we will review each of the above areas and the most recent research findings for the application of this assessment type to vocational rehabilitation with individuals who have psychiatric disabilities. Before addressing specific components of vocational assessment, it is helpful to review recent legislative initiatives and paradigm shifts in professional practice that have affected best practices.

## ADA, the Rehabilitation Act Amendments of 1992, and Vocational Assessment

The Americans with Disabilities Act and the Rehabilitation Act Amendments of 1992 have had a major influence on best practice in assessment of individuals with severe disabilities, including serious mental illness. These laws have occurred in conjunction with a major shifts in the fundamental role and purpose of vocational evaluation and assessment. The ADA mandates equal access to participation with reasonable accommodations provided as appropriate. Likewise, the Rehabilitation Act Amendments of 1992 shifted eligibility consideration to include a presumption of employment potential and required vocational rehabilitation agencies to provide *clear and convincing evidence* if determining service ineligibility.

The Rehabilitation Act Amendments are clear that existing information, to the extent it is available, be utilized in the process and that assessment not be a tool for denying or delaying access to services. The Senate Conference Report on the Rehabilitation Act Amendments of 1992 specifically states that assessments should not be duplicative, "unnecessary" or "irrelevant." Information gathered for any comprehensive assessment is limited "specifically to information that is necessary to develop a program of services." The Conference Report indicates that this information should come, as much as possible, from existing data and not contracted for again if it already exists. Since the majority of individuals with serious mental illnesses have extensive and lengthy histories, including multiple assessments and evaluations of their psychiatric and psychosocial status, best practice indicates these records should be used rather

duplicating the process. These amendments also encourage "preliminary assessment that may include the provision of rehabilitation goods and services" such as supported employment (VCU, 1993). That is, the amendments sanction and recommend the use of situational, *in vivo* assessment after rapid placement.

Assessment practices must change as the concept of reasonable accommodation is extended to the practice of vocational assessment (Thomas, Bowers, Batten & Reed, 1993). Job analysis, for example, has been altered as a result of ADA. Job analysis is a method of identifying the essential functions that make up a job and describes the knowledge, skills and abilities required by workers for successful job performance. It summarizes job content, job requirements and the job context. Due to the ADA, job analysis must now include an assessment of workplace accessibility and reasonable accommodation needs and availability as well as an analysis of the outcomes of a job task, not merely the *method* of task performance (Thomas, Bowers, Batten & Reed, 1993). Studies are needed to examine the effect that accommodation strategies have on the reliability and validity of vocational assessment approaches. Assessment professionals should identify reasonable accommodations within the evaluation process and accommodate those aspects of the disability that will negatively impact the testing performance. This may include making adjustments to the physical environment in which evaluation is conducted as well as the social environment or the actual evaluation process.

## Situational Assessment Practices

A situational assessment is an evaluation of vocationally-related skills within the environment where the skills will actually be used. The closer the evaluation environment is to the target environment, the more valid the results of the situational assessment. This is very important since situational assessments have been correlated with employment outcomes (Cook, Jonikas & Solomon, 1992). Despite being the preferred method of evaluation of individuals with psychiatric disabilities among vocational rehabilitation counselors surveyed nationally (Hursh, Rogers & Anthony, 1988), most research on the psychometric properties of situational assessment have been methodologically unsophisticated (Bond & Friedmeyer, 1987). There are very few validity studies of situational assessment of individuals with psychiatric disabilities in community employment settings (hospital and institutionally based studies are of limited value in generalizing to a community focus).

In general, it appears that longer frames of situational assessment have greater predictive validity than shorter periods of time (i.e., five wks. vs. 13 wks. vs. five months) (Soloff & Bolton, 1969, Bond & Friedmeyer, 1987). Watts (1978) reviewed situational assessment literature and concluded that ratings of social relationships, response to supervision and enthusiasm were predictive of return to work but task competence was not. Similarly, Anthony & Jansen (1984) identified three work skill categories: getting along, doing the job, and being dependable as predictive of work success; the most important variable is interpersonal dimension.

McKenna (1993) advocates the use of behavior rating scales in work settings, noting that behavior rating scales have a high degree of objectivity and behavioral specificity and when applied appropriately, can be used to effectively rate both positive and negative behaviors. The setting, the environment, and the other people involved in the work task should be considered and observed as part of the rating process. Otherwise the assessment may produce results that are myopic or misleading.

Bond & Friedmeyer (1987) developed and field tested a behavior rating scale using a sample of 84 members in a psychosocial rehabilitation program. Staff rated four dimensions of work performance in either a prevocational crew (40 subjects) or transitional employment (44 subjects) between three and eight months after admission. The behavior rating scale consisted of four dimensions that included work readiness (attendance, grooming, control of inappropriate behavior), work attitudes (initiative, acceptance of responsibility), interpersonal relations, and work quality and performance (accuracy and productivity). These researchers reported that use of the full scale (all four dimensions combined) rather than subscales provided the best results and distinguished the group of people who were competitively employed from the prevocational and unemployed groups, as well as the TE group from the unemployed group. These researchers urge caution in the use of situational assessments, noting that, based on their analysis of the data, situational assessment may be more useful for identifying individuals who are definitely not ready for work than selecting those who will succeed. Finally, these researchers observed that the work environment (paid, competitive or TE employment vs. prevocational) affected the situational assessment by affecting motivation and work enthusiasm (i.e. individuals being paid for their work were more motivated than those in prevocational settings).

Rogers, Sciarappa & Anthony (1991) conducted a study to develop and test a method for conducting situational assessment. Their situational assessment process included: a structured exploration and vocational interview, the provision of an optimal work evaluation environment and observation and rating using a Work Adjustment Skills Scale (WASS) and an Interpersonal Skills Scale (ISS). Optimal work evaluation environments for each individual were determined through the use of a scale (Optimal Work Environment Evaluation (OWEE) that surveyed vocational history, likes and dislikes and successes and failures. The WASS and ISS showed good inter-rater and test-retest reliability. Rogers, Sciarappa and Anthony found the situational assessment process predicted unemployment better than employment.

Schultheis & Bond (1994) used the Job Performance Evaluation Form (JPEF) which was adapted from the instrument used by Bond & Friedmeyer (1987). Four subscales — work readiness, work attitudes, interpersonal relations, and work quality and performance — were assessed. They found that situational assessment ratings of work behaviors actually declined over time. They tied this to the absence of an emphasis on finding competitive jobs in the program studied. Additionally, Laird and Krown (1991) noted that sheltered workshop staff were more severe judges of performance than were community employers or the consumers themselves.

The Work Personality Profile (WPP) (Cook et al, 1992) is a behaviorally-oriented work assessment designed for use in a work adjustment program. It is scored on eleven primary scales and five factor scales. The five primary subscales are task orientation, social

skills, work motivation, work conformance and personal presentation. The WPP was correlated with cognitive ability on the General Aptitude Test battery, and also mildly correlated with vocational interest on the U.S. Employment Service Interest Inventory and did not correlate at all with the 16 Personality Factor. There was poor inter-rater reliability, and they recommend two observers be used with this instrument.

The Griffiths Scale (Griffith, 1975, Laird & Krown, 1991), is another tool for rating employee skills in situational assessment. Skills rated include work skills, relations with peers, acceptance of supervision and work attitudes. The scale has been normed on psychiatrically disabled populations and found useful in predicting job retention (Watts, 1978).

## Best Practice Indicators for Using Situational Assessments

Based upon the literature review, best practice in situational assessment includes:

- An evaluation environment that is the actual work environment or approximates the goal environment as closely as possible.
- An evaluation environment that optimizes the individual's evaluation performance.

- Situational assessment is better at predicting who is not ready for vocational goal attainment rather than predicting who will be successful at vocational goal attainment.
- Situational assessment should use multi-dimensional factors, especially those factors having to do with interpersonal relationships and skills.

## Functional Assessment Practices

The concept of functional capacity within vocational rehabilitation is fundamental to the practice of functional assessment. Without an identifiable deficit in functional capacity, the need for rehabilitation services does not exist (Brown, Gordon & Diller, 1983). Rehabilitation makes two basic assumptions about functional skills in vocational rehabilitation. Functional assessment, although often confused with situational assessment, is a distinct process. Functional assessment determines an individual's capacity for functioning, where situational assessment addresses the particular environment in which functioning occurs. Functional assessment may be a component of situational assessment or may be a separate process.

Functional assessment, as used in vocational rehabilitation, is used to measure an individual's functioning at entry into services and as an aid to the development of an IWRP. Functional assessment is often used in research as an outcome measurement, i.e. improvement in functioning after the provision of rehabilitation services (Smith & Ford, 1990). Functional assessment should measure not only the individual skills or behaviors, but also the environmental strengths and deficits that will need to be modified to facilitate vocational rehabilitation (Cohen & Anthony, 1984; Dion & Anthony, 1987). Functional assessment is used in a person-centered approach (Cohen & Anthony, 1984) to help people obtain a better understanding of their skills as related to their goals. This can help change individual's perceptions about how much control they have over their environments and goals. Vaccaro, Pitts, and Wallace (1992) note that there is no definitive instrument, interview process or data source available for functional assessment in psychiatric vocational rehabilitation. The functional assessment process must be flexible enough for measuring the variability in course and outcomes of individuals. They recommend a functional assessment process that is multidimensional, closely tied to the vocational goal, and interdisciplinary.

Liberman (1982) categorized five different kinds of assessment techniques to assess functional social skills. These include:
- self-report
- interviews
- *in vivo* observation
- role playing
- permanent products (pen and paper measures)

The same methods can be used for functional assessment not only of social skills but of intellectual (filling out job applications) and physical (dressing for interviews) skills. An important part of a good functional assessment involves identifying whether the skill deficit is an acquisition problem (i.e., the person doesn't currently have the skill) or an application problem (the person has the skill but can't or isn't using it) (Cohen & Anthony, 1984).

Dellario, Goldfield, Farkas & Cohen (1984) present evidence that functional assessments can be usefully conducted even when individuals are exhibiting very symptomatic behaviors. These researchers conclude that the level of general skill performance can't be

assumed from the level of apparent symptom disturbance. In fact, they conclude, symptom management itself may be a functional skill to include in a comprehensive assessment process. These researchers note the interactive nature of the functional assessment process, both in terms of the shared responsibilities and expertise of the counselor and client, and also the relationship of the assessment process to the rehabilitation process.

Flesher (1990) notes that a brief functional assessment can take place anywhere and gives the evaluator some useful information in a brief period of time. Assigning an instrumental task, e.g., *please get a cup of coffee*, can allow a counselor to assess: a) the ability to follow instructions; b) the ability to concentrate or pay attention to task; c) the ability to learn new tasks and remember routines; and, d) the ability to sustain motivation.

The vocational functional assessment should link the elements of functioning to a larger functional goal. Cohen and Anthony (1984) identified ten critical elements of effective functional assessments for persons with serious mental illness:

1. Relate to the overall rehabilitation goal
2. Should include a resource assessment
3. Be individualized
4. Assess strengths as well as deficits
5. Be comprehensive
6. Involve the individual in the process
7. Behaviorally define the skills that are present and are deficient
8. Include the unit of measurement
9. Be conducted *in vivo* whenever possible
10. Be ongoing

## Functional Assessment Approaches

The Assessment of Occupational Functioning (Watts, Kielhofner, Bauer, Gregory & Valentine, 1986) is a functional assessment tool based on the Model of Human Occupations. It consists of a semi-structured interview and a series of five-point Likert scale items. Test-retest and inter-rater reliability rated at above minimal acceptable levels. However, the instrument was unable to make sufficient, stable judgments about

individual variables such as values, personal causation, roles, habits or skills. It was developed for institutional populations versus community populations.

The MFNA (Multi-Function Needs Assessment) (Werner & Michaels, 1987, Werner, 1993), assesses 13 areas of functioning, one of which is work/school, leisure. It provided two types of information: amount of assistance needed to perform a function (1 = no ass., 5 = total ass.) and the frequency of occurrence of a function. Lower scores indicate higher functioning. The best predictors of functioning were the subscale scores in work/school and leisure. Werner (1993) notes that complex functioning is more difficult than basic functioning to measure. This instrument was also based on institutional rather than community practice.

Wallace (1986) identified six functional assessment instruments that were noted to be effective for persons with psychiatric disabilities:

• The Katz Adjustment Scale (Katz & Lyerly, 1963). The KAS includes an instrument to be completed by a significant other (KAS-R) that assesses psychopathological and interpersonal behaviors. The other instrument (KAS-S) is completed by the individual and assesses performance of socially-accepted activities. The advantages of the KAS are its psychometric properties which make it a good research tool and its usefulness as a general screening tool. Its disadvantages include that it doesn't provide detailed enough information to construct a good rehabilitation treatment plan, it assesses broad areas of functioning rather than specific and it doesn't identify the causes of inadequate skill performance.

• The Social Adjustment Scale (Weissman et al, 1971) is composed of 42 items that yield average performance scores in six social instrumental roles. One of these roles is work. The advantages of the SAS is that it provides specific information relevant for the development of a rehabilitation treatment plan. The disadvantage is that it requires a trained interviewer, raising the cost and inconvenience of its use.

• The Community Adaptation Schedule (CAS) (Burnes & Roen, 1967) is an instrument consisting of 34 subsections including employment and work potential. It is a self-report instrument of 212

items. Also measured are behavior, affect and felt desire for change. The advantages of the CAS are that it was designed for community rather than institutional use and it is good for rehabilitation service planning. The disadvantage of the instrument is that its psychometrics are not well documented and it may be influenced by socially desirable answers on the part of the respondent.

• The Life Skill Assessment (Farkas, 1980, Farkas, Rogers & Thurer, 1987) was designed for institutional use and contains 21 items. It has good inter-rater reliability and reliably discriminates those who are discharged and successful in the community.

• The Independent Living Skills Survey (ILSS) (Wallace, Kochnowicz & Wallace, 1985) assesses nine areas of skills including job seeking. The psychometric properties for the job seeking area were lower in reliability than other parts of the instrument.

• The Community Living Skills Scale (Smith & Ford, 1990) is unique in that it was developed by consumers at a psychosocial rehabilitation agency. Smith and Ford note that the consumers were very reluctant to develop a scale that focused on behaviors rather than feelings. However, after learning that a behaviorally-measurable scale was what is valued in outcome research, the consumers agreed to focus on that area. The finished instrument had four sub-scales rating personal care, socialization/relationships, leisure/activities and vocational skills. As a whole, the instrument demonstrated acceptable reliability on both the whole scale and subscales (including vocational). Because it is a self-report scale, the authors recommend another rater observe the functional level to increase efficacy.

## Best Practices in Functional Assessment

Based upon a review of the literature, best practice in using functional assessment in the vocational

rehabilitation of persons with serious mental illness includes:

- Determine the purpose of the assessment and request an assessment instrument and process that meets the purpose.
- Tie the information requested and the focus of the functional assessment closely to the vocational goal.
- Involve the consumer in the assessment process and use the assessment process to facilitate ownership of the goals and rehabilitation process.
- Functional assessment measurements and results should be observable, measurable and concrete.

- Functional assessment should not be used as a permanent rating
- Functional assessment can be used as an outcome measurement
- Functional assessment in vocational rehabilitation should be specific enough to assist in the formulation of a rehabilitation service plan.
- Reassess frequently.

## Standardized Vocational Batteries

Developers of testing batteries, recognizing the time and financial constraints of vocational evaluators, have concentrated on the construction of testing batteries that include several hands-on assessment measures, traditional psychological tests and work samples. These batteries were created to maximize the amount of information provide in a minimal amount of time (Cook, Bond, Hoffschmidt, Jonas, Razzano & Weakland, 1992). Recently, Cook & Razzano (1992) questioned whether work sample batteries reliably predict job readiness of individuals with psychiatric disabilities. Early studies (Rosen, Clark & Kivitz, 1977, Wehman, 1976) found weak or inconsistent correlations between measures of perceptual and motor skills and measure of employment potential. Halpern, Browning & Brumer (1973) and Wehman (1976) identified social skills and emotional adjustment as variables that might effect the evaluation process and the prediction of work readiness, not work readiness itself.

Anthony & Jansen (1984) reviewed research indicating that standardized pen and paper psychological tests (i.e. personality measures) and IQ measures may not be valid indicators for persons with serious mental illness. Tests that measure ego strength (i.e. situational flexibility) and self-concept in the role of worker were identified as the best predictors of employment outcomes, not standard measures of personality and psychopathology such as the MMPI. To address these concerns, subsequent researchers have suggested using

work samples (Anthony & Jansen, 1984), extended assessment/evaluation periods (Bond & Dietzen, 1993), vocational behavior checklists (Cook, et al, 1991) and multidimensional testing batteries (Fortune & Eldredge, 1982, McCarron & Dial, 1975) to more effectively assess vocational potential.

Cook, et al. (1992) reviewed the relative merits of vocational testing batteries with individuals with serious mental illness. While recognizing the usefulness of the information regarding psychological or emotional health when making decisions about job placement, they urge caution. Several commonly identified standardized vocational batteries are available.

- McCARRON-DIAL WORK EVALUATION SYSTEM (McCarron & Dial, 1972). This battery provides information about verbal-spatial-cognitive ability (WAIS-R, Stanford-Binet, Peabody Picture Vocabulary Test, and/or Wide Range Achievement Test), sensory, motor and emotional functioning (Bender-Gestalt, Haptic Visual Discrimination, McCarron Assessment of Muscular Development [fine and gross motor], Observational Emotional Inventory, MMPI and House-Tree-Person) and integration/coping skills (Street Survival Skills, Dial Behavior Rating Scale). It is a standardized, multi-dimensional battery. Fortune & Eldredge (1982) found weak to moderate significant relationships between vocational factor scores and employment outcomes. They questioned the usefulness of the McCarron-Dial as a sole means of assessment. Cook & Razzano (1992) examined the ability of the McCarron-Dial battery to predict employment status and hourly salary at six and twelve months after testing. Recognizing that demographic and socioeconomic factors such as age, gender, education, and ethnicity may interact with the prediction of employment, they controlled results for these factors. Data was gathered from 221 McCarron-Dial assessments conducted by a PSR agency assessment unit. They found weak but significant relationships between vocational factor scores and employment status. The higher the factor score the higher the likelihood of employment. The factor score was also related to rate of pay. However, when factors such as sex, education, minority status and age were controlled, the vocation factor score fell below .05 level of significance. The two remaining significant variables were years of education and the length of time the individual had been receiving rehabilitation services. The vocational factor score continued to predict rate of pay, even in the multivariate analysis. Cook and Razzano (1992) conclude that the McCarron-Dial is a better predictor of rate of pay than employment status.

- The VALPAR COMPONENT WORK SAMPLE SERIES (Brandon et al, 1975) was originally designed to assess members of the general population who had suffered industrial accidents. Assessment information provided by the Valpar is centered on 16 different work samples ranging from measurement of small tool dexterity and range of

motion to evaluation of independent problem solving and integrated peer performance. Special norming for individuals with serious psychiatric disabilities has not been reported.

- The JEWISH EMPLOYMENT AND VOCATIONAL SERVICE SYSTEM (JEVS) (Jewish Employment and Vocational Service, 1973; Kulman, 1971), THE SINGER VOCATIONAL EVALUATION SYSTEM (Gannaway & Caldwell, 1971), TESTING ORIENTATION AND WORK EVALUATION IN REHABILITATION (Institute for the Crippled and Disabled, 1967) and the VALPAR system (Brandon, Button, Rastatter & Ross, 1975) are frequently used in vocational rehabilitation of individuals with psychiatric disabilities. These work samples may have some benefits, but there are many drawbacks to their use with persons with serious mental illness. The work samples are typically quite brief and individuals who are psychiatrically disabled may not perform consistently over time. Research has not been done to develop work sample techniques that are valid and reliable in predicting the vocational capacity of individuals with serious mental illness (Hursh, Rogers & Anthony, 1988)

While the use of vocational testing batteries is ubiquitous in the practice of vocational rehabilitation, their usefulness for individuals with serious mental illness has not been well studied. Those research projects that have examined the issue have found weak to non-significant results. Best practice indicates that vocational test batteries be used to answer specific questions only and not be used as the primary or sole assessment tool in planning rehabilitation services.

## Conclusion and Recommendations

Vocational assessment differs from diagnostic and eligibility assessments in an important way. Diagnostic and eligibility assessments gather information to categorize a person into a pre-existing schema (by diagnosis of eligibility criteria). Vocational assessment should gather information to address skills and competencies needed to adapt to daily living requirements (Werner, 1993). This creates an assessment process that is less stigmatizing and stereotyping, because the person is not succinctly

labeled (Cohen & Anthony, 1984). Vocational assessment should focus upon identifying the skills needed to work by asking two basic questions:

- What can the person do now? (Behavior as a tool)
- What does the person need? (Behavior as an end)

and should include information regarding:

- the individual's pool of knowledge and level of applied functioning (i.e. what information do they have, how able are they to access the information and use it. What learned behaviors (skills) do they have and to what extent are they able to or are actually using them?).
- the vocational goals and career objectives that the individual will and will not extend effort to achieve.

- the range of behaviors exhibited by the individual and the positive and negative influences these behaviors have upon vocational performance

*(Brown, Gordon & Diller, 1983)*

# References

Anthony, William, & Jansen, M. (1984). Predicting the vocational capacity of the chronically mentally ill: Research and implications. *American Psychologist, 39*: 537-544.

Berven, N. (1984). Assessment practices in rehabilitation counseling. *Journal of Applied Rehabilitation Counseling. 15*: 9-14, 47.

Bond, G., & Dietzen, L (1993). Predictive validity and vocational assessment: Reframing the question. In R.L. Gueckuf, L.B. Sechrest, G.R. Bond and E.C. McDonel (eds). *Improving Assessment in Rehabilitation and Health*. Newbury Park, CA: Sage Publications. pp 61-86.

Bond, G., & Friedmeyer, M. (1987). Predictive validity of situational assessment at a psychiatric rehabilitation center. *Rehabilitation Psychology, 32*: 99-112.

Brandon, T., Button, W., Rastatter, C. & Ross, D. (1975). The Valpar work sample system. In A. Sax (ed), Innovations in vocational evaluation and work adjustment. *Vocational Evaluation and Work Adjustment Bulletin. 8(2)*: 59-63.

Brown, M., Gordon, W., & Diller, L (1983). Functional assessment and outcome measurement: An integrative review. In Pan, Backer & Vash (Eds) *Annual Review of Rehabilitation*. New York: Springer. pp 93-120.

Burnes, A. & Roen, S. (1967). Social roles and adaptation to the community. *Community Mental Health Journal, 3*:153-158.

Cohen, B, & Anthony, W. (1984) Functional assessment in psychiatric rehabilitation. In Halpern & Fuhrer (eds), *Functional Assessment In Rehabilitation*. Baltimore: Paul Brookes, p79-100.

Cook, J., Jonikas, J., & Solomon, M. (1992). Models of vocational rehabilitation for youths and adults with severe mental illness: Implications for America 2000 and ADA. *American Rehabilitation*, Autumn; 6-11, 32.

Cook J., & Razzano, L (1992). Natural vocational supports for persons with severe mental illness: Thresholds supportive competitive employment program. In L. Stein (ed), Innovations in mental health services (23-42). *New Directions for Mental Health Services, 56, Winter*. San Francisco: Jossey-Bass.

Cook, J., Bond, G., Hoffschmidt, S., Jonas, E., Razzano, L, & Weakland, R. (1992) *Assessing Vocational Performance Among Persons with Severe Mental Illness*. Thresholds National Research and Training Center on Rehabilitation and Mental Illness, Chicago, Ill.

Cook, J., & Rosenleigh, T. (1991). *Predicting Employment in the Community Among Persons with a Psychiatric Disability*. American Psychological Association Annual Meeting. Cincinnati, Ohio.

Dawes, R., Faust, D., & Meehl, P. (1989). Clinical versus actuarial judgment. *Science, 243*: 1668-1674.

Dellario, D., Goldfield, E., Farkas, M., & Cohen, M, (1984) Functional assessment of psychiatrically disabled adults. In A.S. Halpern & M.J. Fuhrer (eds), *Functional Assessment in Rehabilitation*. Baltimore: Paul Brookes. pp. 239-252.

Dion, G. & Anthony, W. (1987). Research in psychiatric rehabilitation: A review of experimental and quasi-experimental studies. *Rehabilitation Counseling Bulletin, 30*: 177-203.

Farkas, M. & Anthony, W. (1989). *Psychiatric Rehabilitation Programs: Putting Theory into*

*Practice*. Baltimore, MD: Johns Hopkins University Press.

Farkas, M. (1980). *The effects of training psychiatric staff in human relations and programming skills: Developing a rehabilitation model for chronic clients during deinstitutionalization*. Unpublished Doctoral Dissertation. Boston University.

Farkas, M., Roger, E., & Thurer, S (1987). Rehabilitation outcome of long-term hospital patients left behind by deinstituionalization. *Hospital and Community Psychiatry, 38*: 864-870.

Flesher, S. (1990) Cognitive habilitation in schizophrenia: A theoretical review and model of treatment. *Neuropsychology Review, 1*; 223-246.

Fortune, J., & Eldredge, G. (1982) Predictive validity of the McCarron-Dial Evaluation System for psychiatrically disabled sheltered workshop workers. *Vocational Evaluation and Work Adjustment Bulletin*, Winter; 136-141.

Gannaway, T. & Caldwell, T. (1971). The Singer/Graflex vocational evaluation system. In A. Sax (ed) Innovations in vocational evaluation and work adjustment. *Vocational Evaluation and Work Adjustment Bulletin, 4*: 41-42.

Griffiths, R. (1975) Vocational guidance conducted with psychiatric patients. *Bulletin of the British Psychological Society, 28*: 427-436.

Halpern, A., Browning, P., & Brumer, E. (1973). Vocational adjustment of the mentally retarded. In M.J. Began & S.A. Richardson (eds) *The Mentally Retarded and Society: A Social Science Perspective*. Baltimore: University Park Press.

Hursh, N., Rogers, E., & Anthony, W. (1988). Vocational evaluation with people who are psychiatrically disabled: Results of a national survey. *Vocational Evaluation and Work Adjustment Bulletin*, Winter.

Institute for the Crippled and Disabled (1967). *Tower: Testing, Orientation and Work Evaluation in Rehabilitation*. NY: Author.

Jewish Employment and Vocational Service (1973). *The Development of Time and Quality Norms for the Philadelphia JEVS Sample System*. Philadelphia: Author.

Katz, M. & Lyerly, S. (1963). Methods for measuring adjustment and social behavior in the community: I, Rationale, description, discriminative validity and scale development. *Psychological Reports, 13*: 502-535.

Kaufert, J. (1983). Functional ability indices: Measurement problems in assessing their validity. *Archives of Physical and Medication Rehabilitation, 64*: 260-267.

Kulman, H. (1971). The Jewish employment and vocational service work sample battery. In A. Sax (ed) *Innovations in Vocational Evaluation and Work Adjustment Bulletin, 4*: 25-27.

Laird, M., & Krown, S. (1991) Evaluation of a transitional employment program. *Psycosocial Rehabilitation Journal, 15*: 3-8.

Leconte, P., Sitlington, P. & Hinton, L. (1993). Evolving policy paradigms and legislative implications for vocational assessment services. In Fry & Garner (eds) *Sixth National Forum on Issues in Vocational Assessment*. Menoniaonie, Wisconsin-Stout.

Liberman, R. (1982). Assessment of social skills. *Schizophrenia Bulletin, 8*: 62-83.

Marrone, J., Horgan, J., Scripture, D. & Grossman, M. (1984). Serving the severely psychiatrically disabled client within the vocational rehabilitation system. *Psychosocial Rehabilitation Journal, 8(2)*; 5-23.

McCarron & Dial (1972). *McCarron-Dial Work Evaluation System: Evaluation of the Mentally Disabled -- A Systemic Approach*. Dallas, TX: Common Market Press.

McCarron & Dial (1975). *McCarron-Dial Work Evaluation System*. Dallas: Common Market Press.

McDaniel, R., & McClanahan, M. (1993). Selecting vocational evaluation tools. *Sixth Annual Conference on Vocational Assessment*. University of Wisconsin-Stout.

McKenna, M. (1993). Using behavioral rating scales as part of vocational assessment. *Sixth Annual Conference on Vocational Assessment*. University of Wisconsin-Stout.

Rogers, S. Sciarappa, K, & Anthony, W. (1991) Development and evaluation of situational assessment instruments and procedures for persons with psychiatric disability. *Vocational Evaluation and Work Adjustment Bulletin*, Summer: 61-67.

Rosen, M., Clark, G., & Kivitz, M. (1977). *Habilitation of the Handicapped: New Dimensions in Programs for the Developmentally Disabled*. Baltimore: University Park Press.

Russert, M. & Frey, J. (1991). The PACT vocational model: A step into the future. *Psychosocial Rehabilitation Journal, 14*: 7-17.

Practice in Vocational Assessment and Evaluation

Rutkowski (1990). *Integrating Community Support Programs and Vocational Rehabilitation.* Presentation at 1990 Speakers Series on Supported Employment and Psychiatric Rehabilitation. Department of Psychology (UPU), Indianapolis, IN.

Schultheis A., & Bond, G. (1994). Situational assessment ratings of work behaviors: Changes across time and between setting. *Psychosocial Rehabilitation Journal.*

Smith, M., & Ford, J. (1990). A client-developed functional level scale: The community living skills scale (CLSS). *Journal of Social Service Research, 13*: 61-84.

Smith, F. & Schuster, D. (1993). *Building consensus: The interdisciplinary council on vocational evaluation and assessment.*

Soloff, A., & Bolton, B, (1969). The validity of the CJVS Scale of Employability for older clients in a vocational adjustment workshop. *Educational and Psychological Measurement, 29*: 993-998.

Tashjian, M.D., Hayward, B.J., Stoddard, S., & Kraus, L. (1989). *Best Practice Study of Vocational Rehabilitation Services to Severely Mentally Ill Person: Policy Studies Associates, Vol.1*, p.15-21.

Thomas, S., Bowers, C., Batten, D., & Reed, B. (1993). Assessment of accessibility needs. *Sixth Annual Conference on Vocational Assessment.* University of Wisconsin-Stout.

Urofsky, S. (1993). The potential within us. In Fry & Garner (eds) *Sixth Forum on Issues in Vocational Assessment.* Menonianie, WI: Materials Development Center, University of Wisconsin-Stout.

Vaccaro, J., Pitts, D., & Wallace, C. (1992) Functional assessment. In R.P. Liberman (ed) *Handbook of Psychiatric Rehabilitation,* MacMillan; pp. 78-94.

Virginia Commonwealth University (1993). *PL 102-569: The Rehabilitation Act Amendments of 1992.* Winter.

Wallace, C (1986) Functional assessment in rehabilitation. *Schizophrenia Bulletin, 12*: 604-630.

Wallace, C., Kochnowicz, N., & Wallace, J. (1985). *Independent Living Skills Survey.* Unpublished manuscript, Mental Health Clinical Research Center for the Study of Schizophrenia. W. LA VA Medical Center.

Watts (1978). A study of work behavior in a psychiatric rehabilitation unit. *British Journal of Social and Clinical Psychology., 17*: 85-92.

Watts, J., Kielhofner, G., Bauer, D., Gregory, M., Valentine, D. (1986). The assessment of occupational functioning: A screening tool for use in long-term care. *The American Journal of Occupational Therapy, 40*: 231-240.

Wehman, P. (1976). Vocational training of the severely retarded: Expectations and potential. *Rehabilitation Literature, 37*: 233-236.

Weissman, H.N., Seldman, M., & Ritter, K. (1971). Changes in awareness of impact upon others as a function of encounter and marathon group experiences. *Psychological Reports, 28(2)*; 651-661.

Weiner, H. & Michaels, P. (1987). *Multi-Function Needs Assessment: Adapted version.* Kaneoke, HI: Hawaii State Hospital.

Weiner, H. (1993). Multi-function needs assessment: The development of a functional assessment instrument. *Psycosocial Rehabilitation Journal, 16*: 51-61.

# Chapter 5

## Best Practices in Work Readiness and Work Adjustment Programs

Work adjustment has a long and cherished history within the field of vocational rehabilitation. Dating back to the earliest literature on the practice of vocational rehabilitation, the concept of work adjustment has served as *the* dominant theoretical model. Pruitt & Rubin (1986) define work adjustment as:

> A treatment/training process utilizing work or work related activities to create an understanding and appreciation for the meaning, value and demands of work; to modify or develop appropriate attitudes, personal characteristics and work behavior, and to develop functional capacitites as required to assist individuals toward their optimal level of vocational development.
>
> *(p. 312)*

A number of common characteristics associated with work adjustment programs may be identified. First, skill development and symptom management/remediation are the primary purposes of these programs. Behavior modification, role-playing, behavioral rehearsal, and token economies are frequently reported interventions in work adjustment programs. Second, these programs are typically of a time-limited duration (e.g., 90 days-6 months) with little or no job placement/development, or follow-up services provided. Third, these programs are frequently located in, or affiliated with, an inpatient facility (e.g., state hospital, psychiatric hospital), psychiatric treatment center, or a sheltered workshop. Finally, work adjustment programs typically involve sub-contract work, with participants receiving wages at or below minimum wage, and their wages paid by the rehabilitation program, rather than the employer.

The use of work adjustment for persons with serious mental illness served by the federal-state rehabilitation program is well established. Tashjian, Hayward, Stoddard, and Kraus (1989) reported that work adjustment training was the service most frequently received by the clients sampled in their study. Work adjustment training, along with work maintenance were the two most frequently provided services for clients of the federal-state VR system. O'Brian (1993) advocates the provision of work adjustment and work orientation services, particularly for people whose psychiatric disability is significantly interfering with their ability to pursue concrete rehabilitation goals. He identifies the need for mental health treatment, values clarification, and assistance with goal setting prior to providing formal vocational rehabilitation services.

## Models and Approaches of Work Adjustment

Lysaker and Bell (1995) describe a work adjustment program that was implemented in a VA medical center. Sixty-eight individuals participated in a 26-week work placement program. Participants were placed into a variety of positions within the medical center (e.g., escort service, purchasing office, pharmacy and medical administration) where they worked between 10 and 20 hours per week. The report fails to indicate whether the participants were financially compensated for their work. In addition to working, the participants attended weekly semi-structured support group meetings.

Utilizing computer-assisted instruction, Brieff (1994) describes a classroom-based work adjustment program that was implemented in a New York State psychiatric facility. In this program, residents of the facility attended classes one to five times per week and averaging between four and 20 hours per week. Upon referral by their treatment team, residents received a comprehensive diagnostic screening that included standardized educational testing and computer aptitude testing. Based upon this assessment, residents were generally assigned to either a vocational computer training program that emphasized advanced computer applications or a general education program that strengthened basic academic skills. The report also indicates that a transitional

employment component was available to qualified applicants. However, this element was not described.

While reports on the use of traditional, sheltered workshops and rehabilitation facilities emphasizing the use of light assembly and other sub-contract work are prevalent within the vocation rehabilitation literature (c.f., *Vocational Evaluation and Work Adjustment Bulletin*), recent research reports on its application specific to individuals with serious mental illness are rare (Bond, 1992; Gilman, 1987; Kasser, Davey, & Ryan, 1992; White-Ilg & Wright, 1989). In contrast, transitional employment is characterized by time-limited job placements, an emphasis upon skill development, and agency-controlled jobs, and represents the predominant model of work adjustment for this population. Finally, the use of mobile work crews and enclaves have also been reported sporadically in the literature.

## Outcome Studies on Work Adjustment

Exhaustive reviews of the efficacy of work adjustment applications for persons with serious mental illness have appeared in the literature (Anthony & Jensen, 1984; Bond, 1992). Consistently, these reports have reported marginal outcomes for participants in terms of job placement, job retention, or future earnings. Assessment of various worker traits, work readiness, and work aptitude has been a predominant area of outcome research among investigators reporting the use of traditional work adjustment and sheltered workshop programs. Summarizing these findings, Trotter Minkhoff, Harrison, and Hoops (1988) state:

> Even where traditional vocational rehabilitation programs exist, however, they

have been markedly ineffective for individuals with severe psychiatric disabilities. Sheltered workshops are a case in point: They do not promote meaningful rehabilitation for the majority of people with psychiatric disabilities, both because the clients are not taught relevant skills and because the tasks performed are often regarded as demeaning. For most individuals with a psychiatric disability, the setting itself increases, rather than diminishes, a sense of stigma, despair, and social isolation... most programs have had limited success in returning clients to competitive employment.

*(pp 27-36)*

## Summary and Conclusions

Research cited in Chapters 4 and 8 of this manual demonstrate rather conclusively that rapid approaches to job placement produce superior employment results when compared to more traditional, gradual or step-down models of job development and placement. In light of this evidence, the practice of traditional work

adjustment services does not appear to represent best practices for most persons with serious mental illness. When work adjustment programs are provided, desired characteristics should include:

1. Work adjustment should take place in settings that are integrated and as close to competitive employment as possible. Use of transitional employment and mobile work crews and enclaves may represent best practices when providing work adjustment services.

2. Work adjustment should be time-limited and planned to build specific vocational skills.

3. Work adjustment appears to work better in inpatient or psychiatric hospital settings, particularly when it is coordinated with community job development and placement programs.

## References

Anthony, W. & Jensen, M. (1984). Predicting the vocational capacity of the chronically mentally ill: Research and implications. *American Psychologist.* *39*: 537-544.

Bond, G., (1992). Vocational rehabilitation. *Handbook of Psychiatric Rehabilitation*, Chapter 11: 244-275.

Gilman, S. (1987). Alternatives to open employment in the community. *British Journal of Occupational Therapy, May.*

Brieff, R. (1994). Personal computers in psychiatric rehabilitation: A new approach to skills training. *Hospital and Community Psychiatry, 45(3).*

Jacobs, Harvey, E., et al.; U California School of Medicine, Los Angeles, (1984). A skills-oriented model for facilitating employment among psychiatrically disabled persons. *Rehabilitation Counseling Bulletin, 28*: 87-96.

Kasser, T., Davey, J., & Ryan, R. (1992). Motivation and employee-supervisor discrepancies in a psychiatric vocational rehabilitation setting. *Rehabilitation Psychology, 37*: 175-188.

Kates, N., Woodside, H., Gavin, D., O'Callaghan, J., Young, S., Jones, B., & Case, P. (1989). Home employment: A work alternative for persons who are mentally ill. *Psychosocial Rehabilitation Journal, 12*; 66-67.

Lysaker, P., & Bell, M. (1995). Work performance over time for people with schizophrenia. *Psychosocial Rehabilitation Journal, 18(3).*

O'Brien, W. F. (1993). *Psychiatric Rehabilitation Approach: Assisting Individuals with Severe Psychiatric Disabilities into Integrated Employment Opportunities.*

Pruitt, D.G., & Rubin, J.Z. (1986). *Social Conflict: Escalation, Statement, and Settlement.* New York: Random House.

Tashjian, M.D., Hayward, B.J., Stoddard, S., & Kraus, L. (1989). *Best Practice Study of Vocational Rehabilitation Services to Severely Mentally Ill Persons: Policy Studies Associates, Vol. 1*, p.15-21.

Trotter, S., Minkhoff, K., Harrison, K., & Hoops, J. (1988). Supported work: An innovative approach to the vocational rehabilitation of persons who are psychiatrically disabled. *Rehabilitation Psychology, 33;* 27-36.

White-Ilg, C.A., & Wright, D.A. (1989). Practitioner's point of view: Taking a critical look at traditional programs: Are they effective? *Vocational Evaluation and Work Adjustment Bulletin*, Summer.

# Chapter 6

# Best Practices in Job Development and Job Placement

For many individuals receiving services Vocational Rehabilitation, short-term or time-limited job development assistance and/or job placement assistance are appropriate and effective for successful employment placement and retention. Individuals with persistent mental illnesses need job development and placement efforts to be provided in the context of a comprehensive and long-lasting rehabilitation plan that may include transitional employment, psychosocial rehabilitation, supported employment, and/or supported education. Irrespective of the duration and intensity of services to be provided, effective job development and placement services must share a number of critical features and address a number of issues in the process.

First, establishing an effective network of communication between rehabilitation and the private business sector is critical. Effective job development programs must position themselves as members within the community of business and human resource managers. Second, effective job development agencies must present themselves as a business. From the name of the agency, to the layout of the business cards, to the appearance of the staff, effective job development programs must learn to look, act, and sound like a reputable and successful business. Third, effective job development programs encourage and support consumers to direct their own job development process. Issues regarding direct versus indirect job development assistance, job developer presence on the worksite, and type and location of employment are key decisions around which consumers must be encouraged and supported in making informed decisions. Finally, successful job development programs are those that result in successful, long-term employment retention. Effective and coordinated efforts regarding job placement and development of natural supports and other forms of extended supports are key elements in an effective job development plan.

## Defining Job Development and Placement

Job development is defined as:

Developing job opportunities for hard-to-place rehabilitants is a comprehensive professional service and not simply the solicitation of jobs. Continuing and mutually beneficial relationships with community employers are established through agency services (e.g., selective placement, job modification, adjustment counseling). Job development activities should provide disabled workers with a chance for a career in cooperating firms as opposed to temporary or otherwise substandard employment.

*(Wright, 1980)*

## Employer Issues and Fears Affecting Job Development and Placement

It is important to recognize that employers, like most Americans, may be ignorant (and consequently, intimidated, if not actually discriminatory) about mental illness. The job developer should be aware of, and prepared to respond to, the concerns and fears that employers raise regarding employing workers with mental illness. Likewise, the job developer should be prepared to provide convincing and concise assurances to the employer to allay these concerns and to ensure the establishment of a trusting relationship with the employer.

In a recent qualitative study using open-ended focus groups of rehabilitation professionals and employers, Fabian and her colleagues (Fabian, Lucking, & Tilson, 1995) describe some of the barriers and solutions these individuals identified. Among employers, the most frequently identified barriers were those regarding their own fears, prejudices, and ignorance of the disability. Similarly, rehabilitation personnel also identify employer attitudes as a significant barrier. These

findings corroborate those of Kirszner and his colleagues (Kirzsner, et al., 1994) who surveyed supported and transitional employment employers and found concerns about the productivity, attendance patterns and aberrant behaviors of workers with psychiatric disabilities.

Fabian, et al. (1995), also found that employers identify business climate and cycle conditions such as labor competition, lack of job openings, and the recession as significant barriers to job placement, rather than disease or disability-specific issues. These same employers identified the service qualities of the rehabilitation agency, in terms of follow-up and the agencies' understanding and responding appropriately to employer and company needs, as significant factors in hiring workers with psychiatric disabilities. These findings are also consistent with those of other researchers regarding employers' issues and motivations when hiring persons with mental illnesses (Kirszner et al., 1994).

## The Americans with Disabilities Act and Job Development

The Americans with Disabilities Act provides numerous and significant safeguards for workers with psychiatric disabilities. As job development and placement services are provided, the consumer, rehabilitation counselor, and job developer should have a thorough understanding of the regulations and safeguards of the ADA. A number of resources are available that describe the parameters and processes of the ADA. Some are:

**NIDRR-ADA Technical Assistance Program, Disability and Business Technical Assistance Centers**
Voice and TDD, (800) 949-4232
URL, http//www.icdi.wvu.edu/tech/ada.htm

*Disability Discrimination in Employment Law*
(1996). Robert L. Burgdorf, Jr., Washington, DC: Bureau of National Affairs, Inc., $195
This 1,274-page book offers a detailed discussion of the repercussions of the ADA, including federal legislative, judicial, and regulatory developments.
To order: BNA, Voice, (800) 960-1220
URL, http//www.bna.com.bnabooks

*The Job Developer's Guide to the ADA:*
*Using the ADA to Promote Job*
*Opportunities for People with Disabilities*
(1996). Suzanne M. Bruyère and Thomas P. Golden, Cornell University, (Eds.) St. Augustine, FL: Training Resource Network, Inc., $29
This 102-page book offers a detailed overview of the ADA employment provisions and reasonable accommodations.
To order: TRN, Voice, (904) 823-9800
URL, http//www.oldcity.com/trn

*ADA Information Brief*
Eight briefs: $70
Prepared by the Washington Business Group on Health's
Employer Resource Center on the ADA and Workers
with Psychiatric Disabilities. This series of briefs
provides a variety of information regarding the ADA and
workers with psychiatric disabilities.
To order: Washington Business Group on Health
ATTN: Ann Makowski
777 N. Capitol Street, Suite 800
Washington, DC 20002, (202) 408-9320

## Disclosure and its Implications for Job Development

An important factor of the job development process is the decision of the consumer to disclose or conceal their mental illness. For many individuals, there is a very real concern about employer stigma and discrimination. This may cause them to seek out more discrete and generic job development strategies. Appropriate supports for these individuals include assistance in self-directed job search activities, resume preparation, and interviewing skill development. Other individuals, particularly those requiring on-site supports, may find direct job development supports to be helpful. To date, researchers have not adequately addressed the influence disclosure has upon job development efforts or job retention. As such, it seems appropriate to allow the issue of disclosure to remain a decision of the consumer, rather than a program requirement. Prior to initiating job development supports, it is critical that the rehabilitation provider have a thorough understanding of the consumer's preferences regarding disclosure. For the individual facing the decision of disclosure there are numerous issues to be considered, including when to disclose, the manner of disclosing, and the potential positives and negatives of disclosing.

| | |
|---|---|
| **When to Disclose** | • during the hiring process<br>• after the job is secured, but before beginning work<br>• after a positive performance pattern has been established<br>• when an accommodation is needed<br>• when a crisis occurs |
| **Whom to Tell** | • the immediate supervisor<br>• a higher-level manager<br>• co-workers<br>• friends in other areas of the company<br>• personnel representatives<br>• Equal Employment Opportunity officers<br>• employee assistance personnel, etc. |
| **How Much and What Type of Information to Provide** | • stating that one has emotional problems vs. mental illness vs. some other label<br>• a psychiatric diagnosis label (e.g., DSM IV diagnosis)<br>• the duration of the condition<br>• the prognosis of the condition<br>• medications, other therapies, or supports used<br>• previous, current, or potential impact of the condition on job performance<br>• changes to the work environment that may be helpful (i.e., accommodations) |
| **Methods of Disclosure** | • Self disclosure<br>• Applicant known to agency as former recipient of services<br>• Disclosure by a supported employment agency on behalf of the applicant |

| Benefits of Disclosure | • Disclosure allows the worker to request reasonable accommodations.<br>• Disclosure allows co-workers to offer personal support.<br>• Disclosure enables a worker to involve an employment service provider, employee assistance program, or other third party in the development of accommodations.<br>• Disclosure allows a worker to choose to have a job coach come to the work site and communicate directly with the employer.<br>• Disclosure may make it easier to come to work during a period of heightened symptoms.<br>• Disclosure may facilitate the recovery process.<br>• One disclosure may encourage another. |
|---|---|
| Hazards of Disclosure | • Co-workers may tease, harass, or otherwise discriminate against individuals known to have psychiatric disabilities.<br>• Co-workers may wrongfully assume that individuals with psychiatric disabilities will be less productive members of the team.<br>• Disclosure may limit one's opportunities for career advancement.<br>• Others may attribute all of one's behavior to his or her psychiatric disability and avoid giving feedback that would allow the worker to achieve improved performance.<br>• Identifying oneself as "disabled" may conflict with one's beliefs or self image. |

(Adapted from *Mancuso, L. 1993.*)

## Best Practice Indicators of Job Development Strategies for Workers with Psychiatric Disabilities

### Maximize Marketing and Public Relations Effectiveness

Much has been written about the need for community rehabilitation agencies to position themselves within the business and economic spheres of their community (Fabian, Luecking, & Tilson, 1995 McLoughlin, Garner, & Callahan, 1987; Verstegen, 1994). It has been consistently suggested that effective community rehabilitation agencies display the following characteristics:

- Involvement in local community and business-related activities, as evidenced by active participation in the Chamber of Commerce, Economic Development Council, Kiwanis, Mayor's Committee on the Disabled, and other similar activities.
- A clear and concise definition of their target market and service line that reflects a customer-driven business orientation.
- Develop and provide employers with assistance and consultation services regarding diversity management, accommodation implementation, and other ADA-related needs of the business community.

Recently, the Matrix Research Institute (Kirszner, Baron, & Donegan, 1994) completed a study of 120 employers located in the Northeast who had used supported employment and/or transitional employment services. These findings provide implications for effective marketing and job development strategies, as well as employer preferences regarding on-site supports and services of the placement agency. A majority of employers (52%) indicated that personal contact, as opposed to mailings and public presentations (Chamber of Commerce, Rotary Club presentations), were preferred marketing and job development approaches. Similarly, these employers indicated that simple, single-focus brochures were more effective than costly multi-media presentations and/or brochures. Finally, these results affirmed those of other researchers regarding the importance of the job developers' professional appearance and their knowledge, however modest, of the business to which they are marketing.

Gervey, Parrish and Bond (in press) recently conducted a qualitative analysis of 12 supported employment programs for persons with psychiatric disabilities. These agencies had been identified by the Rehabilitation Information Exchange programs as exemplary in their provision of supported employment services. Gervey, et al.'s findings describe agencies that are vibrant, embracing many of the best practices in business management:

> Uniformly, the respondents conveyed an energetic and enthusiastic commitment to their programs. Moreover, they demonstrated a keen understanding and sensitivity of the unique problems confronting SE programs for persons with psychiatric disabilities (i.e., SSI disincentives, controversies concerning disclosure, integration of mental health services) and a thorough knowledge of SE models and practices. Their genuine interest in evaluating SE services was evident in their development and use of performance tracking systems which each respondent readily referenced during the survey. The authors were left, therefore, with the impression that these exemplary programs were exceptionally well managed. In many ways, it appeared that exemplary SE programs modeled themselves more closely on business practices, than the typical mental health day treatment program. In other words, these programs were interested in results, and employment outcomes really mattered. Clearly, at least for the programs surveyed, the SE movement brings an invigoration to mental health services, and

renewed hope for its consumers of attaining integration in the community.

> *(Gervey, Parrish and Bond, in press)*

## Effective Job Development Strategies

Owing in large measure to the emergence of supported employment in the early 1980s, a renewed approach to job development strategies have appeared in the vocational rehabilitation literature during the past decade (Shafer, Parent & Everson, 1988; Verstegen, 1994). These efforts have emphasized the importance of responsive marketing (Kotler, 1975; Shafer, et al., 1988) over a sales approach to job development. In this approach, the job developer acknowledges two clients: the individual seeking employment and the potential employer. The job developer must strive to develop long-term and trusting relationships with both clients, ensuring the continued provision of ongoing service while maximizing customer satisfaction. The benefits of this dual-client approach to job development has been identified to include greater placement success, greater consumer involvement in the job development and placement process, and greater respect and operating efficiency for the job placement agency (Verstegen, 1994).

Verstegen (1994) describes three primary approaches to job development, including cold-call, referral, and the use of a job development advisory committee. The following table summarizes the implementation steps associated with these approaches.

| "COLD CALL" Model of Job Development | "REFERRAL" Model of Job Development | "JOB DEVELOPMENT ADVISORY COMMITTEE" Model of Job Development |
|---|---|---|
| 1. Survey the community job market.<br>2. Make the initial contact.<br>3. Conduct a survey appointment.<br>4. Make a presentation and proposal; Obtain a hiring decision.<br>5. Hold follow-up meetings. | 1. Prospect for advocates.<br>2. Develop each advocate's employer contacts.<br>3. Approach employers though advocates.<br>4. Job developer contacts employers.<br>5. Survey business.<br>6. Make a presentation and proposal; Obtain a hiring decision. | 1. Hold consulting interviews with key decision makers in target industries to assess employer needs and identify potential advisory committee members.<br>2. Develop ad-hoc job development advisory committee with select employers to obtain recommendations on job development strategies.<br>3. Maintain standing job development advisory committee to obtain ongoing review of strategies and |

| "COLD CALL" Model of Job Development | "REFERRAL" Model of Job Development | "JOB DEVELOPMENT ADVISORY COMMITTEE" Model of Job Development |
|---|---|---|
| | | referrals to other employers. |

To date, little systematic research has been conducted regarding the relative efficacy of these, or other job development approaches.

## Accessing Reasonable Accommodations

For the worker with a psychiatric disability, workplace accommodations can provide a means for juggling the demands and symptoms of their illness while remaining a productive worker. Mancuso (1993), in a comprehensive study of accommodations for workers with psychiatric disabilities, classified accommodations into four primary groupings:

| | ACTION | EXAMPLE |
|---|---|---|
| **Explicit Accommodations** | Both employer and employee are involved and concur on the accommodation | Work schedule is modified (split or shortened) due to employees difficulty in concentrating for extended duration. |
| **Unilateral Accommodations** | Modifications to the workplace implemented by the employer without the direct involvement of the employee using the accommodation. | Job duties are reassigned/ realigned due to supervisor's perception that employee has difficulty interacting with customers. |
| **Self Accommodations** | Modifications to the workplace implemented by the employee without the involvement of the employer. | Employee keeps large water glass or bottle at work station due to medication side effects. |
| **Productivity Accommodations** | Accommodations designed to enhance the productivity and work performance of all workers, regardless of disability. | New process is implemented designed to reduce cycle time or task. |

In general, implementing these accommodations will have little, if any, financial impact upon the employing company. Following are frequently identified accommodations requested by workers with psychiatric disabilities:

- Allowing telephone calls during work hours for support or counseling
- Permitting workers to work at home
- Reserving enclosed office/cubicle work space for workers who have difficulty concentrating
- Permitting water or other liquid refreshment in the work station for the worker experiencing "cotton mouth" side effects of medication
- Allowing schedule changes for medical or therapy appointments

- Job sharing or splitting a shift
- Assigning workers to supervisors with greater understanding of disabilities and accomodations
- Establishing written job instructions and/or written job performance goals

In a recent qualitative study of ten workers with psychiatric disabilities, Mancuso (1993) identified consistent patterns in the manner in which workplace accommodations were conceptualized, identified, and implemented:

1. Workers rarely had direct communication with their employers in which they discussed their psychiatric disabilities.
2. "Explicit Accommodations" in which both the worker and his/her supervisor concurred on the

accommodation being made occurred in only two instances.

3. "Unilateral accommodations" by the employer-in which only the supervisor reported making changes in work assignments, scheduling, or other aspects of supervision due to functional limitations associated with the worker's psychiatric disability-occurred in 4 out of 10 employment situations examined.

4. Four workers described practices they have developed to compensate for or cope with their psychiatric disabilities on the job (of which the employer was unaware). One worker called them "self-accommodations".

5. Although five workers have been assisted by job coaches on site during at least part of their job tenure, participation in supported employment was rarely mentioned as a "reasonable accommodation".

6. Half of the employers (five) described adaptations to the employee's individual work style, abilities, or preferences - not necessarily his or her psychiatric disability. These were viewed by the employer as mutually beneficial because they helped the worker be productive.

7. The accommodation most often cited by the workers was flexible or part-time schedule. The accommodation most often cited by the employers were: 1) modifications in work assignments or other supervisory interventions and 2) flexible or part-time scheduling.

8. Workers described negative social and/or personal consequences from receiving reasonable accommodations in the workplace.

9. Employers, in general, had little awareness of the ADA, and none of them appeared to be making accommodations because they feared legal consequences. Rather, they tended to implement accommodations because they made sense.

In a comparison study of employers and non-employers of workers with psychiatric disabilities, Cook, Razzano, Straiton, & Ross, (1994), found that those employers who were knowledgeable of the worker's psychiatric disability viewed accommodations to be easier to make than those employers who were not knowledgeable. These same employers were also more likely to display attitudes that are supportive of the employment potential and general aptitude of workers with psychiatric disabilities when compared to non-employers.

## Assisting Consumers to Develop and Manage Social Security Work Incentives

Informed planning and coordinated management of financial benefits, especially Supplemental Security Income (SSI) and Social Security Disability Insurance (SSDI), are critical elements of an effective job development and placement program for persons with psychiatric disabilities. A number of researchers have noted consumers' fears about losing entitlements as a major barrier to job placement efforts (Harp, 1994; Tashjian, Hayward, Stoddard, & Kraus, 1989). Prior to the changes in the Social Security Act, many people with disabilities that were receiving benefits were legitimately concerned about the impact work would have on their benefit status. The process of applying for and being determined eligible is a very frustrating experience during which people are often forced to survive in abject poverty for many people, and especially those with psychiatric disabilities. As a result of this experience, an overall lack of information

and understanding on the work incentive programs, and discouragement from others, many people choose not to work or work well below their potential, in order to maintain their benefits and related health care coverage.

In order to assist people in realistically planning for employment, it is imperative that the topic of benefits and entitlements be addressed prior to the job development period. It is essential that consumers and rehabilitation professionals are fully informed about the impact of employment earnings upon their benefits prior to placement. At the point that placement occurs, the changes in current benefits should be discussed. During this time, it is essential to specifically discuss the approximate dollar amount of change in their Social Security checks, food stamps, housing costs, etc. Additionally, it is important to work closely with people to help to establish budgets and savings plans in order to adjust for the financial changes in their different sources of incomes. The Social Security Work Incentives should also be discussed in terms of the effect on benefit checks and in planning long-term vocational needs.

## Job Clubs and Other Psycho-educational Approaches

A common element of job clubs and other group vocational development activities is an emphasis upon skill building and generalization. For example, training consumers in effective interviewing skills, conversation skills, and other social skills has been repeatedly studied. Consistently, these studies have shown that job clubs, both as a job placement process, as well as an ongoing support mechanisms, can be effective elements in the placement and retention of workers with psychiatric disabilities.

Jacobs, Collier, and Wissusik (1992) describe a program they refer to as the Job-Finding Module. This programs is designed to "help persons capable of competitive community employment find work." (pp. 105) Based on the work of Azrin and his colleagues, (Azrin, Flores, and Kaplan, 1975; Azrin & Phillip, 1979; Azrin & Belasel, 1980), this approach provides participants with job-seeking skills training, structured assistance in job seeking, a workplace conducive to the job search, fresh job leads, frequent contact with vocational counselors, daily goal-setting and problem-solving sessions, and a monetary incentive system to encourage consistent participation. In their analysis of the program with a sample of military veterans with psychiatric disabilities, Jacobs and his colleagues (Jacobs et al., 1992) reported that 65% of all participants secured competitive employment or job-related training in an average of 27 days. Unfortunately, insufficient information was provided regarding the characteristics of the participants to ascertain the chronicity of their illness. Similarly, no follow-up information was provided to assess the employment retention of those participants who were placed. Nonetheless, the program developed by Jacobs provides an excellent structure for assisting individuals with long-term mental illness engage in a proactive approach to job securement and has been repeatedly identified as an essential element in other employment support programs. (Danley & Anthony, 1987; Danley et al., 1992)

## Effective Job Placement Strategies of Rehabilitation Counselors

A recent national survey of state agency rehabilitation counselors was conducted to identify effective job placement strategies for workers with psychiatric disabilities (Thomas, Thomas & Joiner, 1993). In this study, a total of 98 counselors were identified and sent a two-page survey listing 24 job placement strategies and seven follow-up techniques. Sixty percent of the surveys were completed and returned. Thirty respondents (N = 30) were chosen to represent a balance of caseload type and rural-urban location. They were asked to participate in a follow-up interview. Among the responses to the written questionnaire, the more high frequently identified placement strategies and the percentage of counselors indicating their use were as follows:

- Training Clients in Finding Job Leads (55%),
- Contracting with Work Adjustment/Placement Programs (57%)
- Arranging and Paying for Job Related Transportation (59%)

Telephone calls and face-to-face meetings were reported with equivalent frequency by more than 80% of the counselors while relatively few of them (less than 45%) reported worksite or direct employer contact and job placement strategies that they used.

## Summary and Conclusions

Best practice in job development services emphasizes the provision of creative, energized, and assertive marketing, networking, and public relations efforts on the part of community rehabilitation agencies. The importance of adopting a two-client approach to service provision, recognizing the employer and the business community in general, as customers of job development and placement services was identified. The Americans with Disabilities Act provides a number of important implications for the job development process and provides community rehabilitation agencies many opportunities to provide education, technical assistance, and other services related to the ADA and to the business community.

## References

Azrin, N. H., & Besalel, V. A. (1980). *The Job Club Counselor's manual: A Behavioral Approach to Vocational Counseling.* Austin, TX: PRO-ED publishers.

Azrin, N.H., & Philip, R. A. (1979). The job club method for the job handicapped: A comparative outcome study. *Rehabilitation Counseling Bulletin, 23*; 144-145.

Azrin, N.H., Flores, T., & Kaplan, S.J. (1975). Job-finding club: A group assisted program for obtaining employment. *Behaviour Research and Therapy, 13*; 17-27.

Cook, J.A., Razzano, L., Straiton, D., & Ross, Y. (1994). Cultivation and maintence of relationships with employers of people with psychiatric disabilities. *Psychosocial Rehabilitation Journal, 17(3)*, 103-116

Danley, K.S., Anthony, W.A. (1987). The choose-get-keep model: Serving severely psychiatrically disabled people. *American Rehabilitation,* pp. 6-29.

Danley, S., Sciarappa, K.& MacDonald-Wilson, K. (1992). Choose-get-keep: A psychiatric rehabilitation approach to supported employment. *New Directions for Mental Health Services, 53*; 87-95.

Fabian, E.S., Lueking, R.G., & Tilson, G.P. (1995). Employment and job placement issues. *Journal of Rehabilitation, January/February/March.*

Gervey, R., Parrish, A. & Bond, G. (in press). Survey of exemplary supported employment programs for persons with psychiatric disabilities. *Journal of Vocational Rehabilitaiton.*

Howie The Harp (1994). Empowerment of mental health consumers in vocational rehabilitation. *Psychosocial Rehabilitation Journal, 17(3)*, 83-89.

Jacobs, H. E., Collier, R. & Wissusik, D. (1992). The job-finding module: Training skills for seeking competitive community employment. *New Directions for Mental Health, 53; 105-115.*

Kirszner, M.L., Baron, M.C., & Donegan, K. (1994). *Employer participation in employment programs for persons with long-term mental illness: A three year research study of employer involvement in transitional and supported employment.* Philadelphia: Matrix Research Institute.

Kotler, P. (1975). *Marketing for Nonprofit Organizations.* Englewood Cliffs, NJ: Prentice-Hall.

Lustig, C., Chow, L., & Leahey, M. (1986). A conceptual approach to job placement with psychiatric and mentally retarded clients. *Journal of Applied Rehabilitation Counseling, 17(1)*; 20-23.

Mancuso, L. (1993). *Case studies on reasonable accommodations for workers with psychiatric disabilities.* Community Support Program, Center for Mental Health Services and The California Department of Mental Health/California Department of Rehabilitation.

McLoughlin, C.S., Garner, J.B., & Callahan, M. (1987). *Getting Employed, Staying Employed.* Paul H. Brookes Publishing Inc.

Shafer, M., Parent, W., & Everson, J. (1988). *Responsive Marketing by Supported Education Programs.* Unpublished manuscript.

Sink, D. (1987). The impact of applicant disability on personnel managers' evaluative judgerments. *Dissertation Abstracts International, 48(3-A)*; 567.

Tashjian, M.D., Hayward, B.J., Stoddard, S., Kraus, L. (1989). Best Practice Study of Vocational Rehabilitation Services to Severely Mentally Ill Person: *Policy Studies Associates, Vol.1*, p.15-21.

Thomas, T.D., Thomas, G., & Joiner, J.G. (1993). Issues in the vocational rehabilitation of persons with serious and persistent mental illness: A national survey of counselor insights. *Psychosocial Rehabilitation Journal, 16*; 131-132.

Verstegen, D. (1994). *Increasing Employment Opportunities for Individuals with Disabilities through Economic Development: Creating Business and Corporate Initiatives.*

Wright, G.N. (1980). *Total Rehabilitation.* Boston: Little, Brown and Company (Inc.).

# Chapter 7

# Best Practices
# in Supported
# Education

Nearly half of individuals served in community mental health centers are between the ages of 18 and 35 (Bassuk, 1980), and 91% completed high school, with nearly half having attended college (Spaniol, Jung, Zipple & Fitzgerald, 1985). Young adults with serious mental illness have been identified as a particularly challenging population to serve (Unger et al., 1991; Stein & Test, 1982; Harris & Bergman, 1985; Pepper, & Ryglewicz, 1981) with marked deficits in coping skills, independent living skills, interpersonal skills, fragmented social networks, judgment, and self-esteem. For these and other individuals, the ability to effectively access and utilize secondary and post-secondary educational opportunities represents an appropriate and reasonable rehabilitation intervention. Unfortunately, persons with serious mental illness are frequently denied access to educational opportunities due to their illness, or are unsuccessful in their own educational efforts. While the ADA and Section 504 of the Vocational Rehabilitation Act of 1973, as amended, has resulted in the establishment of Disabled Student Services (DSS) on most college campuses, these units are typically poorly prepared to address the unique educational support needs of students with serious mental illness. As noted by Unger (1993), educational institutions frequently do not make assistive services readily available to students with psychiatric disabilities and do not actively encourage these students to pursue or remain in the educational environment.

During the past decade, supported education has been developed as an alternative approach to the rehabilitation of persons with long-term mental illness (Cook, Solomon, Jonikas & Frasier, 1990; Unger,

1990; 1992; Unger, Anthony, Sciarappa, & Rogers, 1991; Stein, Cislo, & Ward, 1992; Wolf & DiPietro, 1992). While the concept of supported education emerged out of the supported employment philosophy of the early 1980s, the value of education within a comprehensive psychiatric rehabilitation model has long been recognized as a critical component.

Supported education has been defined as:

> Education in integrated settings for people with psychiatric disabilities for whom post-secondary education has not traditionally occurred or for whom post-secondary education has been interrupted or intermittent as a result of a severe psychiatric disability, and who, because of their disability, need ongoing support services to be successful in the education environment.
>
> *(Unger, 1990 pp. 33-34)*

Supported education has been identified as a viable rehabilitation alternative for young adults with long-term mental illness for three reasons (Cook & Solomon, 1993). First, as a location of services occurring on college campuses, it meets mental health consumers' preference for non-stigmatizing treatment alternatives. Second, the social milieu of college environments provide age appropriate role models and peers for young adult mental health consumers. Third, career development and access to employment opportunities in non-entry level occupations require the vocational, educational, and social growth that post-secondary educational environments promote.

## Supported Education Interventions

A variety of services and supports may be provided under the general category of supported education. However, consistent with the concept of supported employment, these services have a number of defining elements. First, they are person centered and concentrate on the support of individually-identified goals and needs. Second, these services are typically provided within the context of integrated and generic community environments. Finally, supported education services are provided long term in a flexible and responsive manner. Among the more commonly identified elements of supported education are the following types of services and supports:

- orientation to campus
- assistance with registration/class load
- assistance with selecting classes/class load
- extended time for exams
- change of location for exams
- parking
- note taking, tape recorders
- seating arrangements, modifications

- beverages allowed in class
- peer support
- identified place to meet on campus that feels "safe" before or after class
- incompletes rather than failures if relapse occurs
- time management
- study skills
- special reentry classes (college survival, setting personal goals)

*Unger, 1991*

Other commonly-identified elements of effective supported education are peer mentoring and peer counseling (Unger et al., 1987; Cook & Solomon, 1993; Wolf and DiPietro, 1992; Parten, 1993). These interventions have included using program alumni as peer mentors, facilitating weekly peer support and/or study groups, as well as the utilization of formally-trained peer counselors to provide individual counseling and support.

## Models and Approaches

Supported education has been demonstrated in a variety of program sites, including community colleges (Parten, 1993; Jacobs, 1993), universities (Unger, Danley, Kohn, & Hutchinson, 1987; Stein & Ward, 1992; Sullivan, Nicolellis, Danley, Mac-Donald-Wilson, 1993), psychosocial rehabilitation agencies (Cook & Solomon, 1993; Wolf & DiPietro, 1992; Beardsley, Kessler, & Levin, 1984; Cook, Wessel, & Dincin, 1987), and even clubhouses (Dougherty, Hastie, Bernard, Broadhust, & Marcus; 1992). Three distinct models of supported education have been identified: the self-contained classroom, the on-site support model, and the mobile support model (Unger, 1992).

Self-Contained Classroom. In the self-contained classroom model, students attend special preparatory or "re-entry" classes at a college or university along with other students identified as persons with special needs (individuals with physical disabilities, returning older students, etc.). The curriculum may be remedial,

designed to improve math, reading, studying, coping skills, or to ease the transition to the academic environment through campus survival skills. Cook and Solomon (1993) describes a series of three preparatory courses they developed as part of their Community Scholars Program. These courses focused on the following areas: career clarification and planning, time management, and research and writing. Similarly, Unger and her colleagues (Unger, Danley, Kohn, & Hutchinson, 1987) describe a four-semester sequence of courses that addressed profiling vocational potential, researching occupational objectives, career planning, and mobilizing personal skills and resources. Typically, students attend these courses prior to, or concurrent with, their enrollment in mainstream courses. In addition to participation in these courses, students may also be receiving a variety of other educational supports, including individual counseling, peer support groups, and other supports to be described later.

On-Site Support. The on-site supported model is typified by students being matriculated and mainstreamed within a college or university, attending regular classes, and receiving support services on campus by the Office of Disabled Student Services, or other designated college/university support personnel (Unger, 1991; Parten, 1993). In this model, disabled student services counselors provide an array of educational supports and accommodations similar to those provided to "more traditional" college students with disabilities (e.g., learning disabled, deaf, blind, physically challenged). Typically, mental health services are provided in a coordinated fashion with local community mental health programs and agencies.

Mobile Support. The mobile support model is characterized by the provision of supports from a community-based mental health or community rehabilitation agency in lieu of or in collaboration with the college or university. In this model, the students are supported in the same fashion as that of the on-site support model, although the support agency may provide supports to students at a variety of post-secondary educational institutions throughout the community. Dougherty and his colleagues (1992) describe a mobile supported education program operated by Laurel House, a psychosocial rehabilitation clubhouse program in Stamford, Connecticut. The Laurel House Supported Education Program (SEP) has four main components:

1.  Assessments: A club Supported Education staff person works collaboratively with campus "guidance" staff in utilizing typical assessment tools to determine reading and math skills, writing ability, and the presence of specific learning disabilities. A second component was reviewing each student's social skills and support systems including housing, transportation, employment, and financial resources which might influence academic performance.

2.  Development of Academic and Career Choices: This was promoted by encouraging and supporting

students to access and participate in campus activities such as cultural events, student government, and work-study opportunities. The clubhouse environment was promoted as a tool to facilitate the identification of education and career objectives by affiliation with other members, as well as supported and transitional employment services.

3.  Coordination of Services: The staff of the SEP worked to coordinate community services with campus-based services. Staff members served to facilitate, lead, and advocate on behalf of the students and their changing needs — social, clinical, and educational — much like the typical role of a case manager.

4.  Administration: This SEP was a contractual agreement between Laurel House and the Connecticut Department of Mental Health. An Educational Advisory Committee was established as a means of communication between various groups, as a route to evaluate the programs progress, and modify implementation procedures as necessary. The Committee also served to provide in-service training to school campuses to assist educational staff to understand the project's goals and mental health issues. These trainings were noted to be successful at generating faculty support for the students in the program, assisting in avoiding administrative obstacles, and as an information source for campus resources, such as financial aid, scholarships, and social activities.

Another demonstration of the mobile supported education model is the Community Scholars Program, operated by the Thresholds agency in Chicago (Cook & Solomon, 1993). This program provides a comprehensive array of educational and mental health related supports, including case management, preparatory coursework, individual and group supports, individual counseling, and weekly peer support groups. Services are provided within a strengths-based, person-centered philosophy.

## Outcome Studies on Supported Education

To date, there are few published reports available regarding the efficacy of supported education. In fact, in a recent review of the supported education literature, Cook and Solomon (1993) identified but four published studies (Beardsley, Kessler, & Levin, 1984; Hoffman & Mastrianni, 1992; Unger, et al., 1991; Wolf & DiPietro, 1992). The synthesis of these four studies reveals a number of reliable findings.

First, these reports have demonstrated that students with mental illness can be successful in pursuing post-secondary education, as evidenced by course completion and grade point averages. Wolf and DiPietro (1992), in a report of the supported education program of Laurel House, reported that 75% of the participating students received passing grades, with students averaging grades of B or better in 26 of the 37 courses in which they were enrolled. Similar outcomes were reported by Unger (1993) and Dougherty and his colleagues (1992) who reported an overall GPA for participating students of 3.5 and 3.0, respectively. One potential area of concern may be that of course withdrawal. Dougherty reported a high rate of course withdrawal, approximately one out of every three courses in which students were enrolled. Conflicting data were presented by Parten (1993), who reported drop-out rates that were comparable to that of the general student population. The common reasons for dropping out/withdrawal included illness, fear or inability to deal with college, and family crisis.

A second common, although not consistent, finding is that of enhanced vocational performance as students engaged in paid competitive employment, either concomitant with or following their supported educational endeavors (Beardsley et al., 1984; Egnew, 1993; Unger, 1993). Beardsley and his colleagues (1984) reported a 60% rate of competitive employment among the individuals participating in a supported education program. In an analysis of the Thresholds Community Scholars program, Cook and her colleagues (Cook, Solomon, Yamaguchi, Frazier, Gervain, Kerouac, & Eusebio, 1992) reported that 78% of the 102 participants that were interviewed had reported working while in the supported education program. At the time of the three-year follow-up, 47% reported that they were currently employed. In

comparison, Unger (1993) reporting on the outcomes of four different supported education programs, reported that only 17% of those surveyed reported that they were currently employed. With regard to employment outcomes, supported education participants have reported average earnings between $4.75 and $4.80 per hour while working an average of 21 to 24 hours per week (Cook et al., 1992; Unger, 1993).

Third, increases in students' self-esteem as a result of participation in supported educational programs has been reported. Unger (1993) suggests that the process of achieving a new identity as a college student allows individuals with psychiatric disabilities to gain a socially-valued role. Unger contends that this role assimilation can provide individuals with intrinsic energy and motivation to more effectively manage their illness in order to pursue career goals. Empirical evidence of the effect of supported education upon self-esteem was provided by Cook and Solomon (1993) in their three-year analysis of the Community Scholars program. In this study, participants were assessed at intake and at a three-year follow up. These researchers reported statistically significant increases in students' self-esteem and coping skills. Equally important, these authors reported no significant changes in students' self-reported anxiety level.

Finally, research on supported education has consistently identified the need of ongoing, extended supports for individuals as long as they were engaged in educational pursuits. Cook and Solomon (1993) noted that as students in their Community Scholars program became more successful and stable in their educational endeavors, they required more challenging supports in terms of less obtrusive and more liaison or indirect forms of support. Parten (1993), in an analysis of supported education initiatives within California Community Colleges, reported that continuing students required less staff time and fewer services in order to remain enrolled as compared to first-semester students who were new to the supported education program. However, as noted by Egnew (1993), these students continue to require services that are education-oriented and pro-active in identifying and ameliorating potential education support needs.

## Best Practice Indicators

Based upon the research reports to date, a number of elements have been identified in effective supported educational programs. These elements appear consisten across program model variations and represent critical best practices. First, clear administrative support on the part of the educational institution and coordination with community mental health agencies has been identified as a critical component of effective supported education programs (Dougherty et al., 1992; Egnew, 1993; Hoffman & Mastrianni, 1989; Unger, 1993; Wolf & DiPietro, 1992). Given the ignorance and stigma surrounding mental illness, and its misunderstanding among college and university faculty, these educational institutions must provide clear and unambiguous support for the rightful place of students with mental illness on their campuses. As such, inservice seminars, informational pamphlets, and other educational efforts designed to educate and inform educational personnel is critical (Cook & Solomon, 1993; Wolf & DiPietro, 1993). Effective supported education programs are also typified by both formal and informal agreements between themselves and community mental health agencies regarding their separate roles and responsibilities (Dougherty et al., 1992; Egnew, 1993; Hoffman & Mastrianni, 1989; Wolf & DiPietro, 1992; Unger, 1993). Dougherty and his colleagues (1992) reported developing a multi-disciplinary Educational Advisory Committee to establish communication between different community groups and to create a forum for ongoing progress reports. The authors note that this committee was particularly effective in developing cooperative relationships between the educational faculty and the staff and members of Laurel House, leading to the provision of in-service workshops and fostering faculty support and involvement in the supported education program. In discussing the importance of service coordination for supported education, Unger (1993) sounds a warning,

noting that the success of students with mental illness on college campuses can inadvertently result in community mental health agencies "stepping down" the level of mental health care provided to these individuals or psychiatrists reducing the level of prescribed medication.

A second common element that has been identified in supported education programs is that of peer support and peer counseling (Cook & Solomon, 1993; Wolf & DiPietro, 1992; Unger, 1993). The level and type of support reported varies widely from the simple provision of a "safe place" on campus where participating students may meet before or after class, weekly peer support groups, peer mentors and alumni, and more formalized peer counseling using trained and supervised peer counselors. As noted by Parten (1993), these forms of peer support typically require little, if any, staff support for facilitation.

A third and related element commonly identified in supported education programs has been the provision of services to address the social support and integration needs of students with psychiatric disabilities. Wolf & DiPietro (1992), for example, note most students report continuing difficulties in participating in various social activities and establishing a sense of belonging within the social milieu of the student population. In an effort to address this social isolation, Dougherty et al. (1992), describe the efforts of Laurel House to utilize the social support resources of the clubhouse. These efforts included bi-monthly dinners and celebrations for supported education members, which encouraged peer relations and interactions. However, minimal information has been developed to date on strategies to directly assist supported education participants' access and continued participation in regular, mainstream social functions and campus extra-curricular activities.

## Summary and Conclusions

In spite of the scarcity of published, empirical reports, there is little doubt that supported education has been identified and valued as an alternative approach to the recovery process for young adults with mental illness.

Recent system-wide initiatives such as those taken by the California Community Colleges provide clear directives that colleges and universities can accept and accommodate the unique educational needs of students with long-term mental illness. However, a variety of research questions remain to be addressed. Most notably, does supported education result in enhanced vocational outcomes for students? To date, preliminary data, based on small samples and brief follow-ups, provide tentative support. Second, which of the three identified models of supported education aisre more effective? Finally, what is the specific nature of

supports required by students, what educational and demographic variables influence these support needs, and how does the nature of support change over time? The development of information in response to these and other related questions are essential as supported education continues to develop as an institutional alternative for meeting the rehabilitative needs of individuals with long-term mental illness.

# References

Bassuk, E. L. (1980). The impact of deinstitutionalization on the general hospital psychiatric emergency ward. *Hospital and Community Psychiatry, 30:623-627.*

Beardsley, C., Kessler, R., & Levin, I. (1984). Education for the young adult client. *Psychosocial Rehabilitation Journal, 8(1)* 44-52.

Cook, J., Bond, G., Hoffschmidt, S., Jonas, E., Razzano, L, & Weakland, R. (1992) *Assessing vocational performance among persons with severe mental illness.* Thresholds National Researhc and Training Center on Rehaibitation and Mental Illness, Chicago, Ill.

Cook, J., & Solomon, M. (1993). The community scholars program: An outcome study of supported education for students with severe mental illness. *Psychosocial Rehabilitation Journal, 17(3);* 83-98.

Cook, J.A., Solomon, M.L., Jonikas, J.A., & Frasier, M. (1990). *Thresholds supported competitive employment program for youth with severe mental illness.* Final report to the U.S. Department of Education (Grant #G008630404). Washington, DC: Office of Special Education and Rehabilitation Services.

Cook, J.A., Solomon, M.J., Yamaguchi, J., Frazier, M. Gervain, M., Kerouac, J. & Eusebio, E. (1992). *The Thresholds community scholars program: Preliminary evaluation.* Chicago, IL: Thresholds Research and Training Center.

Cook, J.A., Wessell, M.E., & Dincin, J. (1987). Predicting educational achievement levels of the severely mentally ill: Implications for the psychosocial program administrator. *Psychosocial Rehabilitation Journal, 6(1),* 23-37.

Dougherty, S., Hastie, C., Bernard, J., Broadhurst, S. & Marcul, L. (1992). Supported education: A clubhouse experience. *Psychosocial Rehabilitation Journal, 16(2),* 91-104.

Egnew, R. C. (1993). Supported education and employment: An integrated approach. *Psychosocial Rehabilitation Journal, 17(1).*

Harris, M., & Bergman, H. C. (1985). Networking with young adult chronic patients. *Psychosocial Rehabilitation Journal. 8:* 28-35.

Hoffman, F.L. & Mastrianni, X. (1992). The hospitalized young adult: New directions for psychiatric treatment. *American Journal of Orthopsychiatry, 62(2),* 297-302.

Hoffman, F. L., Mastrianni, X. (1989). The mentally illstudent on campus: Theory and practice. *Journal of American College of Health, 38;* 15-20.

Jacobs, E. (1993). Students, staff and community: A collaborative model of college services for students with psychosocial disabilities. *Psychosocial Rehabilitation Journal, 17(1),* 200-209.

Parton, D. (1993). Implementation of a systems approach to supported education at four community college model service sites. *Psychosocial Rehabilitation Journal, 17(3),* 171-187.

Pepper, B., & Ryglewicz, K.H. (1981). The young adult chronic patient: Overview of a population. *Hospital and Community Psychiatry, 32:* 463-469.

Shepard, L. (1993). School Daze. *Psychosocial Rehabilitation Journal, 17(1),* 7-10.

Spaniol, L., Jung, H., Zipple, A., & Fitzgerald,S. (1985). Families as a resource in the rehabilitation of the severely psychiatrically disabled. In Hatfield & Lefley (eds), *Families of the Mentally Ill.* New York: Guilford Press. p. 167-190.

Stein, L.I., & Test, M.A. (1982). Community treatment of the young adult patient. *New Directions for Mental Health Services, 14:* 57-67.

Stein, C.H., & Ward, M. (1992). The power of place: Opening the college classroom to people with serious mental illness. *American Journal of Community Psychology, 20(4)*, 523-547.

Stein, C.H., Cislo, D.A. & Ward, M. (1982). *Building social networks and enhancing social competence. Final Report:* Office of Program Evaluation and Research, Ohio Department of Mental Health.

Sullivan, Nicolellis, Danley, & Mac-Donald-Wilson (1993). Choose-get-keep: A Psychiatric rehabilitation approach to supported education. *Psychosocial Rehabilitation Journal, 17(1)*, 55-68.

Unger, K.V. (1992). Supported education for young adults with psychiatric disabilities. *Community Support Network News, 6(3)*, 1-11.

Unger, K.V., Anthony, W.A., Sciarappa, K. & Rogers, E.S. (1991). A supported education program for young adults with long-term mental illness. *Hospital and Community Psychiatry, 41(8)*, 838-842.

Unger, K. (1990). Supported postsecondary education for people with mental illness. *American Rehabilitation Summer*, 10-14, 32-33.

Unger, K. (1991). Supported education: Serving students with psychiatric disabilities on the college campus. Office of Special Education and Rehabilitation Services *News in Print (Summer)*, pp. 2-6.

Unger, K.V. (1990). Supported education for persons with mental illness: Definitions and models. *American Rehabilitation, 16(2)* 10-14.

Unger, K.V. (1993). Creating supported education programs utilizing existing community resources. *Psychosocial Rehabilitation Journal, 17(1)*, 11-23.

Unger, K.V., Anthony, W.A., Sciarappa, K. & Rogers, E.S. (1991). A supported education program for young adults with long-term mental illness. *Hospital and Community Psychiatry, 41(8)*, 838-842.

Unger, K.V., Danley, K.S., Kohn, L.,& Hutchinson, D. (1987). Rehabilitation through education: A university-based continuing education program for young adults with psychotic disabilities on a university campus. *Psychosocial Rehabilitation Journal, X(3)*, 35-49.

Unger, K.V., Guest Editor (1993). Special Edition on Supported Education: *Psychosocial Rehabilitation Journal, 17(1)*.

Wolf, J., & DiPietro, S. (1992). From patient to student: Supported education programs in southwest Connecticut. *Psychosocial Rehabilitation Journal, 15(4)*, 61-67.

# Chapter 8

## Best Practice in Supported Employment for Persons with Serious Mental Illness

Supported employment has become the service intervention of choice for the vocational rehabilitation of individuals with severe and persistent psychiatric disabilities. Supported employment gained favor as it became obvious that sheltered workshops do not promote meaningful rehabilitation for the majority of people with psychiatric disabilities. Two primary reasons are that individuals are not taught relevant social and vocational skills and because the tasks are perceived of as demeaning while the setting increases rather than diminishes a sense of stigma, despair and social isolation (Estroff, 1989, Ciardiello, 1981, and Vash 1977). Bond and Boyer (1988) conducted a comprehensive review of traditional vocational services such as sheltered workshops and concluded that most programs have had very limited success in returning

individuals to competitive employment. In a recent survey of vocational rehabilitation counselors, supported employment was cited as the most effective strategy, especially for those individuals most severely affected by serious mental illness (Donaldson-Thomas, Thomas & Joiner, 1993).

The purpose of this chapter is to present the models and research regarding supported employment for persons with serious mental illnesses. This chapter will provide an overview of supported employment, review the models most prevalent in the field, review the relevant research in each model and conclude best practices based upon the research. Best practices will cover program models and development, job coach qualifications and interventions and long-term or follow-along support.

## Defining Supported Employment

Supported employment, as described by Wehman & Moon (1988), represented a radical paradigm shift, calling into question a number of fundamental elements of the vocational rehabilitation process. Supported employment advocates the placement of individuals with minimal prevocational training into community employment with time-unlimited or ongoing support. Supported employment minimizes the role of pre-placement, prescriptive assessment, challenges the traditional concept of readiness and work adjustment, and emphasizes the critical role of ongoing support services. The Vocational Rehabilitation Act Amendments of 1992, while maintaining the definition of supported employment that was first articulated in

the 1986 amendments, provided clarification in defining transitional employment as a model of supported employment as well as defining ongoing support services within the context of supported employment. Supported employment is defined as:

competitive work in integrated settings for individuals with the most severe disabilities:

- for whom competitive employment has not traditionally occurred; or

- for whom competitive employment has been interrupted or intermittent as a result of a severe disability; and
- who, because of the nature and severity of their disability, need intensive supported employment services or extended services in order to perform such work.

Such term includes transitional employment for persons who are individuals with the most severe disabilities due to mental illness."

*29 U.S.C. 706(18)*

These amendments also define extended or ongoing support services as services:

1. Provided to individuals with the most severe disabilities;

2. Provided, at a minimum, twice monthly:
   - to make an assessment, regarding the employment situation, at the work site of each such individual in supported employment, or under special circumstances, especially at the request of the client, off site; and
   - based on the assessment, to provide for the coordination or provision of specific intervention services, at or away from the work site, that are needed to maintain employment stability; and

3. Consisting of:
   - a particularized assessment supplementary to the comprehensive assessment;
   - the provision of skilled job trainers who accompany the individual for intensive job skill training at the work site;
   - job development and placement;
   - social skills training;

- regular observation or supervision of the individual;
- follow-up services such as regular contact with the employers, the individuals, the parents, family members, guardians, advocates, and other authorized representatives of the individuals, and other suitable professional and informed advisors, in order to reinforce and stabilize the job placement;
- facilitation of natural supports at the workplace;
- any other services identified.
  *Public Law 102-569, 106 Stat. 4354*

The conditions and parameters of these ongoing support services are further clarified by the 1992 Amendments as services that:

- are provided singly or in combination and are organized and made available in such a way to assist an eligible individual in maintaining integrated competitive employment;
- are based on a determination of the needs of an eligible individual, as specified in an individualized written rehabilitation program;
- are provided by the designated State (VR) unit for a period of time not to exceed beyond 18 months, unless under special circumstances the eligible individual and the rehabilitation counselor or coordinator agree to extend the time in order to achieve the rehabilitation objectives identified in the individual written rehabilitation program
- are provided by a State agency, a nonprofit private organization, employer, or any other appropriate resource, after an individual has made the transition from support provided by the designated State (VR) unit.
  *Public Law 102-569, 106 Stat. 4353-4355*

## Supported Employment Applications for Workers with Serious Mental Illness

It is important to recognize that supported employment is not a single approach or a single model for the provision of services. In fact, an array of philosophies, orientations, and theories have grown around the provision of supported employment to the extent that it may be difficult for the vocational rehabilitation counselor or case manager to be confident that the services marketed by a provider as supported employment are consistent with identified best practice. Research on supported employment for this population has revealed a number of reliable findings (Fabian & Wiedefeld, 1989):

1. Supported employment approaches designed for the developmentally disabled population work poorly for individuals with serious mental illness. Specifically, an emphasis on skills building and behavior modification may not address the complexity of needs for individuals with serious mental illness.

2. The pattern of job coaching and on-going support is fundamentally different for individuals with serious mental illness as compared to individuals with developmental or serious physical disabilities. For individuals with serious mental illness, job coaching interventions tend to have several peaks over much longer periods of time representing periods of exacerbation of either the illness or coinciding with periods of stress.

3. The population of individuals with serious mental illness is so heterogeneous that it may be difficult to systematize job coaching strategies and duties in the same way programs are able to for individuals with developmental disabilities.

4. Specialized caseloads for vocational rehabilitation counselors are a more effective approach to serving individuals with serious mental illness. More than half of VR counselors believe a specialized case load is effective and of those counselors who have a specialized case load, 81% believe it is more effective than a general case load.

*(Fabian & Wiedefeld, 1989)*

A common criticism of supported employment had been its primary orientation toward individuals with developmental disabilities and other individuals experiencing cognitive or physical limitations. Recognizing the unique needs of individuals with psychiatric disabilities, Danley and Anthony (1987) and others (Anthony, Howell, & Danley, 1984; Fabian, 1992; Fabian & Wiedefeld, 1989; Trotter, Minkoff, Harrison, & Hoops 1988) describe a variety of applications of supported employment that most closely parallels that of supported competitive employment: reports of the use of mobile work crews and enclaves are frequently present within transitional employment programs (Forman, 1988; Shimon & Forman, 1991); and reports of entrepreneurial programs are rare, in spite of a number of manuals on developing consumer-run businesses (Masiello, 1993, Yaskin, 1992).

## Models of Supported Employment

### Choose-Get-Keep

The Choose-Get-Keep approach developed by Anthony and others (1990) emphasizes person-centered goals, a client-environment match, prescriptive assessment, planning and intervention and the development of skills and personal supports for success in community settings. The three program activities are: choosing a job, getting a job and keeping a job; parallel job matching; placement and training/follow-along in traditional supported competitive employment programs (Wehman & Moon, 1988). Anthony and his colleagues distinguish their activities as focusing on the participant or individual's progress rather than the rehabilitation staff's activities.

The model emphasizes careful development of individualized vocational rehabilitation plans listing the specific job site and duties that are terminal goals of rehabilitation, the specific skills and education needed to perform the duties successfully, an inventory of the individual's current skills and education, the teaching techniques used to increase the individual's skills and education and the methods used to evaluate progress.

*Choosing* includes employment goal setting, job development, and decision making. These activities occur prior to or overlapping job placement. Family members and significant others are included in the decision making process after the individual has clarified his/her own goal. The purpose of family inclusion is identified as gauging support and identifying future facilitators and barriers to goal achievement. The choosing activities may require a longer period of time than is generally allotted to this phase of supported employment in other models due to the intense involvement of the participant in selecting a job and the difficulty of the choice process for some individuals with serious mental illness. Danley, Sciarappa, and MacDonald-Wilson state their current data indicates from three weeks to six months is necessary. *Getting* activities include placement planning, direct placement, and placement support. During this phase disability disclosure and education about disclosing becomes an important issue. *Keeping* activities include skill development, service coordination and employer coordination.

There have been few outcome research studies of the Choose Get Keep model developed by Boston University. In one study (Danley, Sciarappa, MacDonald-Wilson, 1992) of 19 participants over a one year period, seventeen were employed at least once, fourteen were employed for a minimum of sixty consecutive days and eight were employed at the end of one year. Unger and Anthony (1991) found that 42% of individuals who completed a four-semester course in choosing and getting a job were either employed or enrolled in training/education after the course, compared to 19% before program participation. Trotter, Minkoff, Harrison & Hoops (1988) provided data from a two-year (1985-1987) study of participants in a supported employment program that followed the tenets of Choose-Get-Keep and included skills building, social skills, symptom management and interviewing

skills. Pre-training periods ranged from seven weeks to four months. 152 people were served with 38 remaining in the program at the time of data collection. Forty individuals completed the program and obtained competitive employment, 74 others left either before completing pre-employment training or after failing to obtain employment after initial job placement. Wallace (1993) finds that the model is particularly suited for younger, less disabled individuals for whom there are long-term career choices. Bond (1992) identifies the strengths of the BU model as being its focus on client choice and notes that this emphasis is missing in many other models. However, he notes that it is an untested assumption that extended prevocational career exploration will lead to better outcomes. What has been shown to date is that career exploration leads to greater satisfaction with choices. However, satisfaction with choices is different than success in employment (Bolton, 1988).

## Accelerated vs. Gradual Placement

While the concept of the *Choose-Get-Keep* has been widely disseminated, there has been some question as to its consistency with the key concepts of "supported employment." As mentioned, Bond (1992) questioned whether the untested assumption that extended prevocational career exploration, as articulated as the *Choosing* phase, necessarily leads to better employment outcomes. A number of recent reports have begun to question the value of this pre-placement component and have demonstrated more rapid approaches to supported employment placement. These have included recent reports from Bond on an accelerated placement program (Bond, Dietzen, & Miller, 1993), the PACT vocational model (Russert & Frey, 1991), and the Individual Placement and Support model (Becker & Drake, 1993; in press). The major distinguishing features between each of these three reports and the *Choose-Get-Keep* model has been an emphasis on *rapid* placement into community integrated employment, a recognition of the iterative function of assessment and its relation to extended supports, and an integration of vocational rehabilitation staff in existing community mental health clinical teams.

Bond and his colleagues (Bond, et al., 1993) provided a comprehensive analysis of two approaches to supported employment; one approach, identified as Gradual

Placement, was designed to typify a sequential and gradual progression to employment while the second approach, identified as Accelerated Placement, bypassed pre-vocational activities and placed clients immediately into employment. Results for 74 clients after one year suggested significantly better employment outcomes for Accelerated participants. More accelerated participants obtained competitive employment than did gradual participant (56% vs. 29% p< .05). Thirty-six percent of the accelerated participants worked at full time positions while 64% worked part time. Accelerated individuals retained employment for a longer period of time than did gradual participants (average of 2.3 months vs. average of 0.8 months). Individuals who completed the programs versus those who dropped out did not differ on most demographic or psychiatric history variables. However, dropouts were more likely than completers to either be receiving SSDI or receiving neither SSI nor SSDI at admission. Follow-up over three years indicated that 56% of the individuals in the Accelerated program were competitively employed, compared to 6% of the participants in the Gradual condition. Thirty-five percent of the gradual participants were still attending prevocational work crew. Compared to controls, more individuals in the accelerated condition worked full time and they had worked significantly more weeks for somewhat higher earning. Finally, when asked of their preferences for an accelerated or gradual approach to job placement, 73% of individuals stated they preferred immediate entry into supported employment. While a number of methodological considerations limit the external validity of Bond's results, they provide preliminary support to suggest that rapid placement into supported employment, with the provision of ongoing supports, may be a highly effective approach.

Lysaker, Bell, Milstein, Goulet & Bryson (1993) studied the impact of direct placement in paying jobs on vocational outcomes for people with schizophrenia or schizoaffective disorder. They found that significantly more subjects assigned to the pay condition participated in work. Subjects in a no-pay condition worked fewer hours and dropped out of vocational services sooner than did paid individuals. Neither severity of symptoms nor entitlements had a significant effect on work, whereas pay did. These researchers also note that concurrent symptoms may have effects on specific

work behaviors, although severity of illness as a global feature was a poor predictor of vocational outcome.

Nichols (1989) evaluated the service patterns of 25 individuals in one of the ten Indiana demonstration projects for an average of 66 weeks after admission to the program. Individuals spent 28% of time in prevocational activities (work adjustment etc.), 19% of time looking for a job, 19% of time in a hold status (medication problems, concerns about social security, requested by CMHC staff), and 36% of time in competitive employment. Nichols found that the length of time spent in the various preparation phases was either unrelated or negatively related to vocational outcomes after controlling for time in the program. Their data does not support extended preparation time as enhancing job retention.

Bond and Dincin (1986) randomly assigned 131 consecutive admissions to either a gradual or an accelerated vocational placement. In the gradual condition individuals were required to stay a minimum of four months in the prevocational work crews before they were eligible for transitional employment. In the accelerated condition individuals went directly into TE placements one month after program admission. At a 15 month follow up 2% of the accelerated participants were competitively employed compared to 7% of the gradual participants. Thirty-five percent of the gradual participants were still attending prevocational work crews. More individuals in the accelerated condition worked full time, had worked significantly more weeks, and had earned somewhat more than the individuals in the gradual condition.

More recently, Bond, Dietzen and Miller (1993), comparing gradual and accelerated supported employment placement, reported that more accelerated participants obtained competitive employment than did gradual participants (56% vs. 29% p< .05). Thirty six percent of the accelerated participants worked at full-time positions while 64% worked part time. Accelerated individuals retained employment for a longer period of time than did gradual participants (average of 2.3 months vs. average of 0.8 months). Individuals who completed the programs versus those who dropped out did not differ on most demographic or psychiatric history variables. However, dropouts were more likely than completers to either be receiving SSDI or receiving neither SSI nor SSDI at admission.

## The Individual Placement Support Model

Drake and his colleagues at the Dartmouth Psychiatric Research Center are currently conducting two research projects on a supported employment model that they have described as the Individual Placement & Support model. The IPS model incorporates parts of the BU model with an emphasis upon accelerated placement and the integration of vocational rehabilitation and mental health staff and functions. Selection criteria (entrance criteria includes a spoken desire to work) and prevocational preparation are de-emphasized while individual preferences and choices are addressed through the development of an ongoing collaborative relationship (that may have existed prior to the beginning of vocational services) and a high level of individualization in service planning and program implementation. Participants engage in a brief educational group, prior to enrollment in the program, to assist them in making an informed choice about whether to participate. The majority of IPS services are provided *in vivo*. The Individual Placement and Support model has been described as:

> ...a team oriented, Community Mental Health Center vocational service that assists persons with severe mental illness in obtaining and maintaining competitive employment. IPS emphasizes client choice *rapid job finding*, competitive jobs, integrated work settings, and follow-along support services. Excluding clients from employment services, extensive initial assessments, and pre-vocational training are de-emphasized.
> *(Becker & Drake, in press, pp. 2)*

Of the models reviewed for this chapter, IPS places the greatest emphasis on integrating the vocational rehabilitation counselor into the supported employment process. Their model encourages very frequent (weekly) meetings with the VR counselor, preferably at sites that will make the counselor familiar to other individuals in the mental health system. Although acknowledging differences in motivation (closure for VR counselors and better community living for psychosocial staff) they focus on the similarity of goals

between the cooperating agencies (helping people get and hold jobs). They recommend and emphasize a great deal of relationship building and improved communication.

In one study (Becker & Drake, in press), a CMHC agreed to close one of two day treatment facilities and to convert the staff positions to IPS employment specialists. Individuals in that program were followed longitudinally and compared to individuals in a traditional day treatment facility in the same CMHC. One-year outcomes indicate that both volunteer and paid jobs increased in the program that converted to IPS. Fifty-five percent of the "high utilizers" of day treatment secured a paid job in the converted program within one year of the program change as compared to only 8% of the day treatment program attendees.

The Individual Placement Model emphasizes the use of integrated systems for effective vocational rehabilitation. Becker and Drake (in press), compared IPS services in an integrated CMHC setting with individuals who received vocational services provided by a private vendor outside of the CMHCs. Placing vocational teams into CMHC teams was reported to facilitate clearer communication and cooperation (Becker and Drake, in press). Research indicates inter-organizational communication difficulties and conflicts are often present when vocational services are provided by a vendor outside the CMHC. Serendipitous findings were that case managers and psychiatrists shifted to a more positive view of the work potential of even very disabled individuals when vocational services were integrated into the CMHC agency mission and the interdisciplinary team.

The Individual Placement Model has been studied most in areas that are comparably small (60,000 - 150,000 people) with mental health systems that are supportive of mental health services research (New Hampshire, Wisconsin PACT). It is not clear whether the model, as designed, would work as well, as designed, in other settings with larger populations or systems with a different orientation. Additionally, the model is very new with many of the studies complete within the past three years, or currently in press or in preparation. The long-term retention rates of IPS are yet to be determined. There is some recent evidence from Test (1991) that vocational success attenuates over time and that rapid placement models, such as the ISP, may have greater initial rather than long term success.

The Individual Placement Model stresses the need to create an employment model that fits the needs of an individual agency, clientele or community. Bachrach (1988), Stein & Test (1985) and Dincin & Witheridge (1985) have all found in their research into the

transplanting of models from one area or agency to another, that adaptation of a part (or parts) of several models may be more beneficial. Bond and Boyer, (1988) and Bond and McDonel, (1991) caution that in creating these new and individualized models, agencies must describe the new model in clear and unambiguous terms, using standard definitions and delineating outcome criteria.

## Enclaves, Work Crews and Businesses

Paid work crews include a variety of paid work opportunities that are organized by rehabilitation agencies. An enclave consists of a group of individuals who work together in a factory or other setting and who are usually trained and supervised by non-handicapped workers (Bond, 1992). Marrone (1993) defines affirmative industries as "a business entity set up for the purpose of employing people with disabilities, usually subsidized heavily by rehabilitation or social services money. In a national survey, Granger (1990) located 142 affirmative industries for persons with serious mental illness - most of these were operated by mental health agencies. Frequently handyman work crews are organized by agencies to use clients for day-labor (Schultheis & Bond, 1994). These approaches have not been studied systematically to date (Bond, 1992), with the exception of a controlled study that showed good outcomes for a program that operated

several affirmative industries (Meisel, McGowen, Patotzka, Madison & Chandler, 1993).

Meisel et al (1993) have preliminary findings for three demonstration projects in California. The Village project is a program where staff have developed an array of employment options using a strategy described as "transitional work sites and employment opportunities (a cafe and catering service, a mini-mart, a bank, a janitorial service and clerical positions)." During the second year of the project the staff shifted to spending more time in finding job placements in the community. Of 203 individuals randomly assigned to the Village or to a control group receiving usual mental health services 52% of Village clients and 7% of controls were employed. Of the 52 Village clients who were working, 20 were competitively employed and 44% of wages earned were from competitive employment.

## Employment Retention and Extended Supports

Recent research has begun to more accurately assess the type and amount of extended supports needed by workers with psychiatric disabilities, following job placement and closure from VR services. Bond, in an extensive review of the supported employment literature (1992), concludes that the role of extended, post-VR closure, employment supports are essential to the employment retention of this population. Bond recommends that for persons with serious mental illness, supported competitive employment might better be described as *place and support* rather than place and train, in recognition of the fact that most individuals require supportive interventions, rather than

instructional interventions in order to maintain employment. Similarly, Cook and Razanno (1992), among others, have challenged the concept of *fading* which has been a hallmark of the *follow-along* phase of supported employment. While Kregel and his colleagues have well documented the gradual and consistent reduction of employment supports for persons with developmental disabilities, (1989), individuals with mental illness typically require a higher level of follow-along services, with more frequent "peaks" in support utilization, due to the cyclical nature of the illness and susceptibility to crisis services. The best model of job coaching support to individuals with serious mental illness is a holistic approach rather than a partitioned approach. Cook and Razanno (1992) suggest:

> ... we may need to re-think at least two fairly standard assumptions of vocational rehabilitation: that clients need support for a time limited period after which they should be closed, and second that support needs fade in a simple linear fashion over time on the job. . . Perhaps a lifelong succession of fadings is a better way to conceptualize the needs of persons with psychiatric disability throughout their employment career.
> *(Cook and Razanno, 1992)*

Studies comparing job coaching intervention time between individuals with developmental disabilities and individuals with psychiatric disabilities has found the job coaching time on the job site was significantly less for those with psychiatric disabilities (Johnson & Rusch, 1990; MacDonald-Wilson, et al 1991). Gervey and Hardin (1993), for example, report an average of

only 60 hours of job coaching during the first seven months of placement. Gervey (1994) suggests that given the relatively smaller percentage of time that job coaches provide on-site supervision, programs may consider hiring more job developers and broadening the role of the job coach to maximize the productivity of this position.

The most frequently cited intervention correlated with employment retention has been on-going support (Cook, Jonikas & Solomon, 1992). Wehman (1992) states that ongoing support occurs "when public funds are available on an ongoing basis to an individual or a service provider who is responsible for providing long-term employment support and when these funds are used for specialized assistance directly related to sustaining employment. Ongoing support can include training of new job skills, working on site as needed, liaison with employers, care-givers and family members, and the development of coping and problem solving strategies. They must occur at least twice a month but may be achieved through phone calls and off-site meetings.

## Research on Employment Retention

Cook & Rosenberg (1994) conducted a logistic regression analysis of outcomes among psychiatric rehabilitation clients and found uninterrupted vocational support was a major predictor of employment status even when controlling for prior work history, client demographics and level of functioning. Cook, Razzano, Straiton and Ross (1994) in analysis of job ending patterns among supported employees with mental illness, reported that employers (vs. clients or staff) made the decision to end jobs in 32% of the placements reviewed, suggesting the critical importance of maintaining employer relations during the follow-up phase. Fabian and Wiedefeld (1989) reported that 69 individuals served in their program worked at least 27.4 hours per week with 47% retaining their job for at least six months. Fabian (1992) conducted a survival analysis of individuals in a place-train model program and found that after six months 59% remained employed. The largest percentage drop-off rate for the entire sample occurred in their first month (16%) and again at 24 months (16%) when only

1/3 of the placed group remained working. Cook and Razzano (1992) report that 81.9% of individuals in their program were employed at some point during the 36 month study period. Finally, Shafer and Huang (1995) report on the supported employment retention rates among 107 participants in their University-based program. These researchers report a median retention rate of first job placements of four months, with approximately 45% of the placed participants retaining employment for six months or more. Post-hoc analysis suggested a positive correlation between employment retention and the age of the participants.

Becker & Drake (1993) point out that most people with severe mental illness need minimal assistance in the area of on-site skill development. Rather, they need frequent, even daily, contact to go over what happened at the job, benefiting from guidance and support that is primarily provided away from the job site and addresses such difficulties as interpersonal problems. They cite the need for ongoing support with peaks and valleys rather than an early peak with subsequent fading.

Dellario, Goldfield, Farkas & Cohen (1984) note that there are two phases to skill learning in rehabilitation. The first is acquisition of the skills, the second is utilization of the skills. The job coach for individuals with serious mental illness is typically focused on appropriate utilization of skills rather than skill acquisition. Fabian & Wiedefeld (1989) emphasize a job coach's support as focusing on interpersonal skill development including appropriate social interactions with coworkers and supervisors. They cite the tightrope that is walked between fading off the job site too soon (person is not confident enough to perform) and staying too long (person remains dependent on the job coach and doesn't form natural supports). Their program provides additional ongoing support through a weekly two-hour work retention group that allows employees to discuss job related issues and problems as well as a job site follow along service.

Very little practical information is included in the psychosocial rehabilitation literature on the development of natural supports. Many articles point out potential sources of natural support but few ideas of how to create it. One article identifies stages in creating natural supports, noting that it is not best practice to leave a person expecting natural supports will develop naturally. The stages that they identify are: observe the work place and living environment and identify those individuals who would appear to be most amenable to providing natural supports; facilitate interactions between the individual and the natural support; create periods of temporary fade to assess the success or barriers of the natural support system; and intervene to address problems in natural supports and then fade off the site leaving natural supports in place. This model was an anecdotal model with face validity and apparent common sense but no confirming data or experimental studies.

## Integrating Supported Employment and Mental Health Services

A major area of research and demonstration of supported employment interventions for persons with serious mental illness has concentrated on the integration of vocational rehabilitation and community mental health services. For example, the PACT vocational model (Russert & Frey, 1991) has been developed as an integration of Assertive Community Treatment (Stein & Test, 1985) and supported employment, and is described as consisting of five program elements: Assessment, Individualized Vocational Treatment Planning, Job Tailoring/

Preparatory Problem-Solving, Adjustment to Employment, and Follow-Along. Russert & Frey (1991) note that clinical data from the PACT model shows PACT clients are employed at a significantly higher rate and a significantly higher level than the national average, with 40% to 50% of PACT clients employed at any given time and 80% involved in vocational programming. Additionally, the Individual Placement and Support model (Becker & Drake, 1993) described previously utilizes an integrated staffing model.

## Supported Employment Personnel Qualifications, Skills, & Competencies

There is general agreement among all research reviewed for this chapter that the employment support needs of individuals with serious mental illness are different than the employment support needs of individuals with developmental or other serious disabilities. The amount, intensity, and topography of employment supports required of this population challenges some of

the established ideas regarding staffing of supported employment programs. Consequently, the qualifications, competencies, and resulting training needs of employment specialists working with this population will be different in some areas as compared to employment specialists working with other supported employment customers.

Anthony and Blanch (1987) found that the relationship developed between an individual and their job coach was especially important as trust and consistency may be primary factors in facilitating the individual's transition to work. Mosher and Burti (1992) emphasize this when they point out that too often the best laid technology fails at the feet of poor interpersonal relationships between provider and receiver of services. Drake and Becker (1993) have found that the most successful employment specialists are assertive, high-energy, task oriented and optimistic. These individuals should be comfortable with doing their jobs in the community rather than in an office. Other qualifications include: knowledge of severe mental illness, including diagnosis, medication, and treatment; a knowledge of a broad array of occupations; an ability to form relationships with and interact with employment; some basic assessment and counseling skills; and an ability to work as part of an interdisciplinary team.

While employment specialists should have some experience working with individuals with serious mental illness, lack of experience should not rule out someone who is otherwise promising. Drake and his colleagues note that the most important qualification is a true and unwavering belief that most, if not all, individuals with serious mental illness can work if the right job and the right supports are found. They encourage agencies to look for: general knowledge and experience in job development; ability to contact and work creatively with employers; and an ability to identify individual's interests, strengths, skills, abilities and needs.

Becker and Drake (1993) also recommend the pairing of job coaches to increase coverage in case of emergencies and to facilitate a staff support system to decrease burnout and stress.

## Summary and Conclusions

Based upon the review of literature the following conclusions regarding the best practices for supported employment are:

- Support interventions associated with employment success tend to be those that are ongoing, not time-limited, and occur in peaks and valleys rather than peaking at the beginning of employment and fading. Best practice indicates that the vocational rehabilitation field may need to re-define on-going support parameters and funding.

- All models of supported employment reviewed in this chapter were more effective in producing competitive, community employment outcomes than sheltered workshops, even when severity of illness and functioning and other demographic characteristics were controlled.

- Better outcomes tend to be associated with accelerated vs. gradual placement into employment.

- Supported employment seems to work better in an integrated setting where recovery from serious mental illness is addressed through treatment of the mental illness and vocational rehabilitation under one administrative umbrella.

- Different models of supported employment may be more or less appropriate to different individuals; i.e. the Choose-Get-Keep model may be most effective for younger, more well educated individuals who are less disabled by the symptoms of their mental illness and have long-range career goals, while the Place-Train model or IPS model may be more appropriate for individuals who are more impacted by the symptoms of their mental illness and are interested in work rather than career.

# References

Anthony, W. (1991). Recovery from Mental Illness: The new vision of services researchers. *Innovations & Research, 1(1),* 13-14.

Anthony, W., & Blanch, A (1987). Supported employment for persons who are psychiatrically disabled: An historical and conceptual perspective. *Psychosocial Rehaibitaion Journal, 11;* 5-23.

Anthony, W., Cohen, M., & Farkas, M. (1990). *Psychiatric rehabilitation.* Boston, MA: Center for Psychiatric Rehabilitation.

Anthony, W., Howell, & Danley, K. (1984). The vocational rehabilitation of the seriously psychiatrically disabled. In M. Mirabi (ed), *The Chronically Mentally Ill: Research and Services.* New York: Spectrum. pp.215-237.

Anthony, W.A., & Blanch, A. (in press). Supported employment for persons who are psychiatrically disabled. *Psychosocial Rehabilitation Journal.*

Anthony, W.A., Danley, K.S.,& Sciarappa, K. (1992). Choose-get-keep: A psychiatric rehabilitation approach to supported employment. *New Directions for Mental Health Services, 53;* 87-97.

Bachrach, L.L. (1988). Defining chronic mental illness: A concept paper. *Hospital and Community Psychiatry, 39:* 463-469.

Becker, D., & Drake, R, (1993) *A Working Life: The Individual Placement and Support (IPS) Program.* New Hampshire: Dartmouth Psychiatric Research Center.

Becker, D.R., & Drake, R.E. (1993). *A working life: the individual placement and support (IPS) program.* New Hampshire: Dartmouth Psychiatric Research Center.

Becker, D.R., Drake, R.E. (in press). Individual placement and support: A community mental health center approach to vocational rehabilitation. *Community Mental Health Journal.*

Bolton, B. (1988). Vocational assessments of persons with psychiatric disorders. In J.A. Ciardiello & M.D.Bell (eds), *Vocational Rehabilitation of Persons with prolonged Psychiatric Disabilities.* Baltimore: Johns Hopkins. pp. 165-180.

Bond, B., & Boyer, S. (1988). The evaluation of vocational programs for the mentally ill: A review. In J.A. Cieardiello & M.D. Bell (eds), *Vocational Rehaibiation of Persons with Prolonged Mental Illness*
(231-263). Batimore: Johns Hopkings University Press.

Bond, Dietzen, L, & Miller, L., (1993) *Accelerating Entry into Supported Employment for Persons with Severe Psychiatric Disabiltiites.* Unpublished Manuscript.

Bond, G. & Dincin, J. (1986). Accelerating entry into trasitional employment in a psychosocial rehabiitation agency. *Rehabilitation Psychology, 31;* 143-155

Bond, G. & McDonel, E. (1991). Vocational rehabilitation outcomes for persons with psychiatric disabilities: An update. *Journal of Vocational Rehabilitation, 1:* 9-20.

Bond, G. (1987). Supported work as a modification of the transitional employment model for clients with psychiatric disabilities. *Psychosocial Rehabilitation Journal, 11(2),* 55-73.

Bond, G. (1992) Vocational rehabilitation. In RP Liberman (ed), *Handbook of Psychiatric Rehabilitaton,* MacMillan; 244-272.

Bond, G. (1992). Vocational rehabilitation. In R.P. Liberman (ed), *Handbook of Psychiatric Rehaibiliaton,* MacMillan 244-272.

Bond, G.R., & Pincini, J. (1986). Accelerating entry into transitional employment in a psychosocial rehabilitation agency. *Rehabilitation Psychology 31(3),* 143-155.

Bond, G.R., Dietzgen, L.L., & Miller, L.D. (1993). *Accelerating entry into supported employment for persons with severe psychiatric disabilities.* Paper presented May 4, 1993

Brown, M. & Basel, D. (1988). Understanding differences between mental health and vocational rehabilitation: A key to increased cooperation. *Psychosocial Rehabilitation Journal, 12:* 23-33.

Ciardiello, J.A. (1981). Job placement success of schizophrenic clients in sheltered workshop programs. *Vocational Evaluation and Work Adjustment Bulletin, 14:* 125-128.

Conley, R. & Noble, J. (1990). Benefit-cost analysis of supported employment. In F.R. Rusch (ed), *Supported Employment: Modes, Methods & Issues.* Sycamore, HI: Sycamore Publishing. pp. 271-287.

Cook, J., & Rosenberg, H. (1994). Predicting community employment among persons with psychiatric disability: A logistic regression analysis. *Journal of Rehabilitation Administration, 18,* 6-22

Cook, J., Razzano, L., Straiton, D., & Ross, Y., (1994) Cultivation and maintenance of relationships with employers of people with psychiatric disabiities. *Psycosocial Rehabilitation Journal, 17*, 103-116.

Cook, J.A., & Razzano, L. (1992). Natural vocational supports for persons with severe mental illness: thresholds supported competitive employment program. *New Directions for Mental Health Services, 56*, 23-41.

Cook, J.A., Jonikas, J.A., & Solomon, M.L. (1992). Models of vocational rehabilitation for youths and adults with serious mental illness. *American Rehabilitation, 6.*

Danley, K.S., & Anthony, W.A. (1987). The choose-get-keep model: Serving severely psychiatrically disabled people. *American Rehabilitation*, pp. 6-29.

Danley, S., Sciarappa, K.& MacDonald-Wilson, K. (1992). Choose-get-keep: a psychiatric rehabilitation approach to supported employment. *New Directions for Mental Health Services, 53*, 87-95.

Dellario, D., Goldfield, E., Farkas, M., & Cohen, M. (1984) Functional assessment of psychiatrically disabled adults. IN A.S. Halpern & M.J. Fuhrer (eds), *Functional Assessment in Rehabilitation* (239-252). Baltimore: Paul Brookes.

Dincin, J. & Witheridge, T.F. (1982). Psychiatric rehabilitation as a deterrent to recidivism. *Hospital and Community Psychiatry, 33(8).*

Donaldson Thomas, T., Thomas G.,& Joiner, J.G. (1993). Issues in the vocational rehabilitation of persons with serious and persistent mental illness: A national survey of counselor insights. *Psychosocial Rehabilitation Journal, 16(4)*, 131-132.

Estroff, S. (1989). Self, identity, and subjective experience of schizophrenia. *Schizophrenia Bulletin, 15(2)*, 189-196.

Fabian, E., & Widefeld, M.S. (1989). Supported employment for individuals with severe psychiatric disabilities: A descriptive study. *Psychosocial Rehabilitation Journal, 13(2)*, 53-60.

Fabian, E., & Wiedfeld, M.F. (1992). Supported Employment for severely psychiatrically disabled persons: A descriptive study. *Psychosocial Rehabilitation Journal, 12(3).* 53-60.

Fabian, E.S. (1992). Longitudinal outcomes in supported employment: A survival analysis. *Rehabilitation Psychology, 37(1).* 23-35.

Forman, J.D. (1988). Sheltered work in a non-sheltered setting. *Psychosocial Rehabilitation Journal, 10*: 19-28.

Gervey, R. & Hardin, M. (1993). *A description of the activities involved in providing job coaching services to persons with psychiatric disabilities.* Workshop presented at the 14th Annual Conference of the International Association of Psychosocial Rehabilitaiton Services, New Orleans.

Isbister, F., & Donaldson, G. (1987). Supported employment for individuals who are mentally ill: program development. *Psychosocial Rehabilitation Journal 11(2)*, 54-54.

Johnson, J.R. & Rusch, F.R. (1990). Analysis of hours of direct training provided by employment specialists to supported employees. *American Journal of Mental Retardation, 94(6)*; 674-682.

Kregel, J., (1989). An analysis of services provided by employment specialists in the individual placement model of supported employment. In P. Wehman and J. Kregel (eds), *Supported Employment for Persons withDisabilities: Focus on Excellence.* Human Sciences Press, Inc.

Lysaker P.L., Bell M.D., Milstein R.M., Goulet J.G. & Bryson G.J. (1993). Work capacity in schizophrenia. *Hospital and Community Psychiatry. 44*: 278-280.

MacDonald-Wilson, K., Revell, W.G., Nguyen N., & Peterson, M. (1991). Supported employment outcomes for people with psychiatric disability: A comparative analysis. *Journal of Vocational Rehabilitation, 1(3)*, 30-44.

Marrone, J., (1993) Creating positive vocational outcomes for people with severe mental illness. *Psychosocial Rehabilitation Journal, 17(2)*, 43-61.

Masiello, P., & Masiello, B. (1993) *A Very Small Business... Going from an Idea to Opening a Shop.* INCube, Inc.

Meisel, McGowen, Patotzka, Madison & Chandler, 1993

Mosher, L., & Burti, L (1992). Relationships in rehaibiation: when technology fails. *Psychosocial Rehabilitaiton Journal, 15*, 11-17.

Russert, M.G., & Frey, J.L. (1991). The PACT vocational model: A step into the future. *Psychosocial Rehabilitation Journal 14(4)*: 7-18.

Schultheis A., & Bond, G. (1994). Situational Assessment ratings of work behaviors: changes across time and between setting. *Psychosocial Rehaiblitation Journal.*

Shafer, M., & Huang, H.W. (1995). Evaluating psychiatric vocational rehabilitation services: A community rehabilitation information system. *Psychosocial Rehabilitation Journal, 18(4)*; 65-72.

Shimon, S.M., & Forman, J.D. (1991). A business solution to a rehabilitation problem. *Psychosocial Rehabilitation Journal, 14(4)*.

Stein, L.I., & Test, M.A. (1985). The training in community living model: A decade of experience. *New Directions for Mental Health Services, 26.* San Francisco: Jossey-Bass.

Test, M. (1991). The TCL model. In R.P. Lieberman (ed), *Rehabilitation of the Seriously Mentally Ill.* New York: Pergamon Press. pp. 153-170.

Trotter, S., Minkoff, K., Harrison, K. & Hoops, J. (1988). Supported work: An innovative approach to the vocational rehabilitation of persons who are psychiatrically disabled. *Rehabilitation Psychology, 33(1)*, 27-36.

Unger, K. and Anthony, W. (1991). A supported education program for young adults with long-term mental illness. *Hospital and Community Psychiatry, 42*: 838-842.

Vash, C.L. (1977). Sheltered industrial employment. *Emerging Issues in Rehabilitation.* December.

Wallace, C. (1993). Psychiatric rehabilitation. *Psychopharmacology Bulletin, 29*, 537-548.

Wehman (1992). *Life Beyond the Classroom.* Baltimore: Paul H. Brooks.

Wehman, P. & Moon, M. (1988). *Vocational Rehabilitation and Supported Employment.* Baltimore: Paul H. Brooks.

Wehman, P. (1986). Supported competitive employment for persons with severe disabilities. *Journal of Applied Rehabilitation Counseling, 17(4)*, 24-29.

Wehman, P., & Kregel, J. (1985). A supported work approach to competitive employment of individuals with moderate and severe handicaps. *Journal of the Association for the Severely Handicapped, 10(1)*, 3-11.

Wehman, P.W., Revell, W.G., Kregel, J., Kreutzer, J., Callahan, M., & Banks, D.B. (1990). Supported employment: An alternative model for vocational rehabilitation of persons with severe neurological, psychiatric, or physical disabilities. In J. Kregel, P. Wehman, M.S. Shafer (eds.), *Supported employment for persons with severe disabilities: From research to practice.* Richmond: Virginia Commonwealth University.

Yaskin, J.C. (1992). Nuts and Bolts: A Technical Assistance Guide for Consumer/Survivor Self-Help Groups. National Mental Health Consumer Self-Help Clearinghouse/Project SHARE.

# Chapter 9

# Best Practices in Transitional Employment

The practice of Transitional Employment (TE) dates back to 1958 when the first transitional employment program (TEP) was created by John Beard at the Fountain House Clubhouse in New York City. Since this origin, transitional employment has merged in practice with many of the more recent applications of supported employment. In fact, transitional employment was identified in the 1986 Amendments to the Vocational Rehabilitation Act as a form of supported employment. More recently, the 1992 Amendments defined transitional employment as:

> ...a series of temporary job placements in competitive work in integrated work settings with on-going support services for individuals with the most severe disabilities due to mental illness. In transitional employment, the provision of on-going support services must include continuing sequential job placements until job permanency is achieved.
>
> (*1992 Amendments to the Vocational Rehabilitation Act*)

Typically, transitional employment programs include time-limited (six-to-nine months) placements in positions that have been negotiated and secured by an agency, usually a clubhouse or community rehabilitation agency. Most transitional employment positions are competitive part-time placements; frequently, a full-time position will be secured by the rehabilitation agency and divided into two 15-20 hour slots. Less prevalent TE offerings are a group or enclave in which groups of six-to-ten persons along with a staff person work at a job site. This allows for individuals with greater support needs to receive additional staff and peer support not normally available in transitional employment. Group placements represented only 16 of the 146 transitional employment

positions reported by psychosocial rehabilitation clubhouse agencies (Macias, Kinney, & Rodican, 1995) Research has identified six key characteristics of transitional employment:

1. Transitional employment positions are located in business and places of work in the community, with diversity in job types necessary to meet the needs of the individuals served by the agency.

2. Individuals working in transitional employment are paid prevailing wages (at least minimum wage) directly by the employer.

3. All transitional employment positions "belong" to the clubhouse or community rehabilitation agency. Formal written agreements between the agency and the employer are in place which identify the roles and responsibilities of the individual worker, the employer and the clubhouse or community rehabilitation agency.

4. Transitional employment positions are part-time, (usually 15-20 hours per week), and time-limited (6-9 months).

5. Eligibility and placement criteria are minimized; the desire to work is considered the most important factor determining placement opportunity.

6. Individuals participating in transitional employment positions are encouraged to remain active in the clubhouse, or other community based activities and groups, when not at work.

(*Macias, Kinney, & Rodican, 1995*)

A central concept of transitional employment is *gradualism*, in which it is anticipated that a person's ability to function will be gradually improved as they move through a series of less restrictive (and more challenging) placements in the process of achieving fuller integration in the community (Bond, 1992; Dincin, 1975). As such, transitional employment can be viewed as a form of work adjustment, providing a series of successive approximations to the world of work in which a number of key variables (e.g., type of work, hours worked per day, length of job) can be controlled to assist the individuals to develop the skills, self-esteem, confidence, and behavioral traits (punctuality, attendance, social skills, etc.) necessary for successful employment.

## Outcome Studies on Transitional Employment

Research regarding the effectiveness of transitional employment in achieving competitive employment has produced conflicting results. Although there are many promising reports, there is too great a tendency to rely on face validity, data derived from short periods of time, and outcomes that infer relationships to eventual competitive employment rather than hard data on employment outcome and length of competitive employment It should be pointed out that this lack of outcome data is not isolated to transitional employment programs, but is indicative of the paucity of empirical evaluation of employment outcomes throughout the rehabilitation field for persons with serious mental illness.

Rutman and Armstrong (1985), in a survey of 114 transitional employment programs, reported that 35% of the participants had "graduated" to competitive employment, while another 16% were in another transitional employment placement. Similarly, Ruffner (1982) reported competitive employment rates in excess of 40% for transitional employment graduates. Malamud (1985), in a follow-up study of members of the Fountain House clubhouse, reported a 33-36% rate of employment among former transitional employment participants. The average duration of employment placement of these individuals was 13 months. Bond and Boyer (1988), in a review of the literature available at the time, sharply criticized transitional employment due to its failure to move clients into regular employment and cited a number of studies to support their argument. In one study conducted in Maryland, competitive employment was observed for only 5% of transitional employment graduates among 28 programs over a 12-month period of time. Similarly, a survey of 24 psychosocial clubhouses found that only 12% were in competitive employment or transitional employment 42 months after clubhouse participation and that an additional 46% were still involved in pre-vocational activities (Malamud & Associates, 1988). Similar to the arguments surrounding accelerated supported employment placement, critics of transitional employment have consistently taken exception to the developmental nature or gradualism of the approach.

This criticism notwithstanding, transitional employment, both clubhouse and non-clubhouse based, represents a viable alternative to mobile work crews, enclaves, or sheltered workshops, while providing individuals with exposure to real work conditions. For individuals not quite ready for competitive employment, transitional employment can provide a bridge between the structure and support of a rehabilitaiton center and the independence and demands of competitive employment. Additionally, there is some evidence that transitional employment is cost effective:

> Ignoring anticipated future benefits from unsupported work, the benefit-cost ratio for transitional employment for consumers with mental illness was at least equal to the average benefit-cost ratio of the job-coach version of supported employment. Factoring in the discounted value of anticipated future earnings from the eventual full-time unsupported work of 20% of the TE participants increases the benefit-cost ratio to more than $6 per dollar spent--a substantial return on the investment.
> *(Noble, 1991, p, 1)*

## Transitional Employment and Clubhouses

The overwhelming majority of literature on how to develop and operate transitional employment programs has been developed by psychosocial rehabilitation agencies known as clubhouses. These clubhouses represent a alternative form of mental health services that emphasizes the importance of peer-to-peer relationships in the therapeutic milieu of mental health treatment. Additionally, these clubhouses in many respects operate like a community center; clients are called members, and members are expected to contribute to the functioning of the clubhouse by helping out in a variety of tasks or activities. These tasks form the work units of the clubhouse, which provide the structure of a *work-ordered day*. Colleagues of Fountain House developer John Beard have been very successful and prolific in establishing explicit criteria and standards for developing and operating clubhouses in the Fountain House tradition. In fact, the International Center for Clubhouse Development (ICCD) provides a vast array of information and materials to assist agencies and groups develop and sustain Fountain House-based clubhouses for persons with serious mental illness.

Assisting members to achieve employment has always been one of the central tenets of the Fountain House model. Transitional employment was developed within the clubhouse model and has lead some to argue that transitional employment should only be provided by clubhouses (Macias et al., 1995). However, as pointed out by Morrone (1993) and various supported employment implementation surveys (Wehman, Kregel, & Shafer, 1989), transitional employment services are also being provided by community rehabilitation agencies as well. This "new breed" of transitional employment, provided outside the context of a clubhouse, is indicative of the creativity and diversity in employment support options that have been spawned as a result of the supported employment initiatives of the 1980s. It may be helpful for the VR counselor, case manager, or consumer seeking employment support services to find out exactly what a program means by TE, mobile work crews, or supported employment when describing their services.

While staunch advocates of the Fountain House model will argue that transitional employment provided outside of the context of a clubhouse is not *real* transitional employment, the debate is largely academic at this time. To date, no known studies have been conducted to evaluate the relative efficacy of clubhouse-based transitional employment versus non-clubhouse-based transitional employment. Until such evidence is accumulated, transitional employment as provided either by a clubhouse or some other community rehabilitation agency (such as a community mental health agency, a supported employment agency, sheltered workshop) should be viewed within the context of the six key characteristics that were previously discussed. The extent to which an agency achieves each of these characteristics is more reflective of its ability to provide transitional employment than the other services (e.g., clubhouse, supported employment, vocational assessment, case management) that the agency may offer.

## Implementing Transitional Employment

Whether providing transitional employment from a clubhouse or another community rehabilitation agency, developing and sustaining transitional employment sites in community employment settings require a number of common activities. One model of developing transitional employment identified three sequential phases: *Finding, Establishing*, and *Maintaining* (Fellowship Foundation, 1983).

### Finding Phase

During the initial finding phase, guidelines regarding the clubhouse-member-employer relationship must be developed, implemented, and followed. Among the guidelines that should be considered are:

- jobs should be at businesses that have been established for at least one year so that members and staff are spared the extraordinary stresses that characterize new ventures while procedures and management stabilize

- regular working hours should be established so that job backup and support can be most available
- if at all possible, jobs should be accessible by public transportation

In rural areas, provisions for transporting workers may have to be developed. In addition, strategies for obtaining jobs should include: building on current relationships and business contacts; sharing the responsibility for job development among all staff and board members; and, educating board members about this function.

## Establishing Phase

The establishing phase of transitional employment is a crucial time when establishing ownership of the transitional employment position occurs. The key process during this time is *education* — of the employer, staff, and consumers. Educating the employer includes familiarizing the organization with the population served and the overall agency program, and keeping regular and frequent communication, not just in the beginning and at times of crisis. For agency staff, education should focus on the dignity of work, and staff role. A key part of the staff role is the learning of the transitional employment job through actual performance and then teaching of the job to the workers involved. Consumer education is focused on learning how TE works, and teaching them specific skills while performing the job.

Recent findings by Matrix Research Institute (Kirszner et. al., 1994) support the importance and delicacy of the educational process and how it needs to be integrated with the ongoing process of establishing quality relationships. They report that supported employment and TE employers:

- did not want to be provided with a great deal of information about mental illness
- experienced considerable job mobility
- did not care about the theoretical and practical distinctions associated with a program model
- a majority preferred to do their own training and supervision of new SE/TE employees.

On the other hand, what they report employers valued most was the promise of support from the agency — responding quickly to emergencies, on-the-job support, and (seemingly contradictory to the above report) assistance with training and preparation. The Matrix study emphasizes the long-term educational and relationship building process. They conclude:

> ... expanding the number of cooperating employers and the number of SE/TE job opportunities for persons with long-term mental illness will require the same painstaking and individual effort that has characterized the slow pace of job development thus far. Individual contacts with employers and a genuine commitment to meet employer's needs long after the initial placement is accomplished will continue to be the key to successful SE/TE job development for persons with long term mental illness.
> *Matrix Research Institute (Kirszner et. al., 1994, p. iv executive summary)*

The establishment phase of TE development is a lengthy one, taking the better part of a year or longer. It is not until several individuals have held a TE job that this phase can be considered complete. Employers develop a strong commitment to the first individual to successfully hold each job and often are reluctant to have the job turn over to a new individual. Likewise, consumers and staff can be reluctant to change. It helps to have a written agreement signed by both employer and consumer, acknowledging the temporary nature of the placement and thus affirming the ownership of the job by the program. This also prevents an individual from claiming unemployment benefits and thus sabotaging the continuity of the placement as was reported by one program. As the time gets close for change, all parties participate in celebrating the success and preparing for the change. A strategy common to developing a new TE that has been very successful is to have the first individual on a new placement be an individual who has a previous successful experience with TE. The experienced consumer can greatly aid in the education and relationship-building process that is key to this establishment phase.

## Maintenance Phase

The third phase of TE development, maintaining TE, is a natural outgrowth of the establishment phase. The education and relationship building activities continue, but consistent support is the primary tool utilized — once again for consumers, staff and employers. As the employer experiences success in the guarantee that the program will meet the productivity needs of the employer, either by the regular worker, backup worker, or a staff person, their involvement and commitment to the program can increase. It becomes necessary during this phase to maintain consistent contact and communication, give public recognition, and explore ways to further involve the employer with the agency. It is at this time that the initial altruism that many employers evidence is reinforced and takes on substance.

During the maintenance phase it is important to focus on staff and worker support as well. Recognition for good work on TE is something that must be communicated regularly at the agency. Staff evaluations must focus on this skill and supervision time be given to help staff refine their abilities. Structural supports are put in place by developing back-up staff and consumers who can help staff manage the TE placement. Daily recognition of success is important in all program areas.

Bilby (1992) describes the purpose and value of the backup coverage commitment to employers as serving to create a relationship with employers in which placement failure is understood to be a part of the TE process. "To sustain the relationship, the program takes on the burden of frequent member changes and unsuccessful starts by covering absences, training each member who tries the job, and bridging the productivity gap between ending and starting members" (p. 72). If the job gets done every day, employers are more likely to assume ownership of the rehabilitation mission, tolerate individual's attempts at work, and recognize the small successes of people attempting employment. This somehow takes the sting out of perceived failures by people, allows staff to celebrate attempts at growth, and validate what Beard, et al. (1982), described as the "right to fail as a part of the legitimate and essential experience for most vocationally disabled members in their effort to eventually achieve a successful work adjustment. ... the opportunity to fail on a job is a part of the total learning experience of working" (p. 46). Therein lies the essential strength of a TE system. It recognizes that individuals have significant work adjustment problems that cannot be separated from job acquisition and learning. Bilby describes this process as struggling repeatedly with adjustment issues and vocational habits, and needing repeated opportunities and support with successive TE opportunities and clubhouse work responsibilities.

## Providing Transitional Employment from a Clubhouse

Beard, et al. (1982), provided a comprehensive discussion of Transitional Employment as a program that evolved from and is inextricably linked to Clubhouse participation. While recent evidence of non-clubhouse-based transitional employment questions Beard's assumption, it is nonetheless informative to review the conceptual basis of the clubhouse and its relationship to providing transitional employment opportunities. Beard, et al. (1982), identifies four central tenets of clubhouses:

- the concept of *membership* and the program belonging to those who participate
- members made to feel on a daily basis that their presence is *expected*

- all program operations are designed to have members work side by side with staff to let members know they are *wanted*
- and all members are constantly reminded that they are indeed *needed*, whether it is to run the snack bar, or to complete a statistical analysis

Staffing at a clubhouse is purposefully insufficient to get the job done without relying on and involving members.

These basic tenets serve as the foundation for the Standards for Clubhouse Programs which are reviewed at each bi-annual International Seminar on the Clubhouse Model. The most recent revision published in 1994 lists 36 standards which were specifically related to the following domains:

- Membership
- Relationships
- Program Space
- Work-ordered Day
- Employment
- Functions of the House
- Funding, Governance and Administration

Among the 250 Clubhouses recognized by the International Center for Clubhouse Development, there is substantial, but not 100%, adherence or ability to adhere to all standards. The agreement is by consensus and the standards, although prescriptive, are continually evolving as are individual clubhouse's ability to implement the standards. Propst (1992) writes that the standards are "highly prescriptive in nature and intent. They are to be taken as a whole. They provide the beginning of an answer to the very broad question: What is a clubhouse?" (p.26).

Assistance in finding independent employment is a responsibility of the clubhouse — both the membership and staff. Bilby (1992) challenges clubhouses to become more focused and aggressive in their efforts to help members obtain and maintain independent employment. Among the activities clubhouses typically provide include helping members prepare resumes, prepare for interviews, and confronting the issue of the impact of competitive employment on public benefits and entitlements. Bilby (1992) identified the need for clubhouses to focus more consistent attention on providing ongoing support to those individuals who have become competitively employed. Staff should be consistently available during hours and days that are accessible to those working full-time. Phone contacts, individual counseling and support groups should be regularly provided during work day evenings and on weekends. Members who are unsuccessful at competitive employment should have the ability to quickly re-enter a transitional employment placement to allow for continuity of work and confidence while they sort out their next vocational step.

## The Work Ordered Day

A central concept of clubhouse-based transitional employment is that of the work ordered day. This concept permeates the clubhouse work units that form the rehabilitative structure of the clubhouse. The implementation of the work ordered day becomes the focus of the clubhouse community and serves to integrate the clubhouse community with TE and the outside world. Behind the concept of the work ordered day are two deeply held beliefs (Beard, et al., 1982). First, a belief in the potential productivity of the most severely disabled psychiatric client; and second, the belief that work, especially the opportunity to aspire to and achieve gainful employment, is a deeply generative and reintegrative force in the life of every human being. These basic beliefs underlie the implementation of best practices in a clubhouse to support the development of transitional employment.

The work unit is the basic structure utilized by clubhouses to organize the work ordered day. A work unit is composed of staff and members who share in the tasks that meet specified needs of the clubhouse membership. Common examples of work units are:

food service, research, clerical, education, etc. Waters (1992) says that "the work of a clubhouse should be based on assisting people in meeting their basic human needs: needs such as being wanted and needed, needs that range from food and shelter, to acceptance and recognition, to employment and relationships" (p.43).

The opportunity for transitional employment placement becomes integral to the work units by design. Units are given ownership and management responsibility of specific TE placements. The message of "I need your help to work this TE placement" is just an extension of the message " I need your help to prepare this meal, or get this statistical report on TE finished." Decisions on who will get a TE position are centered in the unit, made by staff based on real member input from observable unit work habits. Members are involved in compiling TE statistics, not just because they are needed to do the work, but because it is their right of ownership of their clubhouse that they know the outcomes of their labors.

A problem often reported by clubhouses is finding enough work for all the members. Waters (1992) sees four major contributing factors in not having enough work. These are: work not being related to the needs of the members; the clubhouse not having enough TE positions; staff unclear about their roles (which will be covered in the next section under professional roles in TE); and agencies not willing to let members take on work tasks — especially true when the clubhouse is part of a larger parent organization.

Clubhouses run the risk of becoming "work-dominated rather than work-ordered" (Vorspan, 1992, p.53). This can occur when the concept of the work ordered day is misunderstood and clubhouses institute such practices as requiring participation or levels of productivity, telling members that they must be in their work units, or requiring members to leave the clubhouse for the day if they don't work. When policies such as these are implemented, the voluntary nature of the member involvement and the ownership of the clubhouse can be compromised and work ceases to be celebrated and

enjoyed. Waters (1992) succinctly communicates the relationship of the clubhouse to TE when he states:

> Work units are only as strong as our TE programs and vice versa. TE gives validity to the work of the unit and prevents the stagnation that permeates programs that have no clear avenue to the larger community. Work units and TE working in harmony are the lifeblood of the clubhouse, and they keep the oxygen called hope surging in the veins of our clubhouse communities.
>
> *(p. 44)*

Members who are on TE and return to spend a portion of their work day in the clubhouse epitomize the inter-relationship between transitional employment and work units. They not only serve as role models for the potential of persons with mental illness, but also reinforce the importance of the work at the clubhouse. By coming back, they make the connection to transitional employment real and grow in their own work adjustment by extending their work day.

## Best Practice Indicators

In summary, the provision of transitional employment for persons with serious mental illness has a long and established history that is closely linked to the clubhouse movement. Recently, however, transitional employment has also begun to be provided as a service separate from a clubhouse, by community mental health or rehabilitation agencies. Transitional employment is characterized by part-time employment in community-based integrated work settings that are established by a formal agreement between the support agency (clubhouse, community rehabilitation agency) and the employer. Workers are paid prevailing wages (minimum wage or better) and will stay in a placement for six-to-nine months before moving on to another transitional employment position, or competitive employment.

TRANSITIONAL EMPLOYMENT BEST PRACTICE INDICATORS:
* Placement decisions reflect consideration of the desire to work as the single most important factor determining placement opportunity. TE is seen as

a right of membership and open to any member who desires to work.
* Placement opportunities will continue to be available regardless of success or failure in previous placements
* TE is located at the employers place of business and provides contact with non-handicapped employees.
* Selection and training of members on TE is the responsibility of the TE program managers, not the employer. (selected employees must be able to meet the normal work requirements of the employer)
* Members are paid directly by the employer at the prevailing or minimum wage, whichever is higher.
* The TE program evidences a wide variety of job placement opportunities.
* T.E. placements are part-time, generally 15-20 hours per week, and limited to about 6-9 months in duration.
* Program ownership of the T.E. placements is evidenced through longevity of placement availability and utilization by numerous members.

- T.E. placement managers make regular and frequent visits to the job site -- not just for crisis and training visits.
- There is evidence of adequate staff and member backup for each placement.
- Members show a history of multiple placements prior to and resulting in independent employment.

BEST PRACTICE INDICATORS OF THE CLUBHOUSE IN FOSTERING T.E.:
- The clubhouse day is work-ordered, with staff and members involved in all aspects of clubhouse operation including administrative tasks.
- Clubhouse evidences ownership of the T.E. program and it's placements via management of TE placements by clubhouse staff and members, not T.E. specialists.
- Evaluation of work readiness is based on T.E./unit work habits, not external evaluation.
- Members on T.E. placements continue involvement in clubhouse work units.
- Members are given equal access to all clubhouse opportunities and have the right to choose the way they utilize the clubhouse and the staff with whom they work.
- Employers evidence familiarity with and pride in the clubhouse, and its programs. They are helped to learn about and enjoy relating to persons with SMI.
- Clubhouse members and staff prepare reports on T.E placement, wages, and other outcomes, and make these reports available internally and externally.
- The clubhouse space conveys a sense of identity to staff, members, and community, and is designed to facilitate the work-ordered day. All space is shared by members and staff.
- The work done in the clubhouse is exclusively the work generated by the clubhouse to operate and enhance the clubhouse community.
- All work in the clubhouse is designed to help members regain self-worth, purpose and confidence.

- The clubhouse assists and supports members to secure, sustain, and upgrade independent employment.
- The clubhouse evidences a commitment to promoting and offering member educational opportunities.
- The clubhouse provides a program of normalizing adult social and recreational activities during weekend, evening and holidays.

BEST PRACTICE INDICATORS IN CASE MANAGEMENT/ REHABILITATION COUNSELOR ROLES:
- The Clubhouse controls its own membership intake process which is voluntary, and allows for immediate reentry unless members pose a danger.
- Formal clubhouse meetings evidence an openness to both staff and members with no formal staff only or member only meetings where program decisions and member issues are discussed.
- Staff function as generalists and are sufficient in number to engage the membership in the work-ordered day, yet small enough in number to make carrying out their responsibilities impossible without major member involvement.
- External appointments do not interfere with T.E. work hours.
- Case management tasks delegated to generalist role of clubhouse staff/unit or, if case management is not done by generalist model, then unit/case manager communication is unit based.
- Case management is the responsibility of the staff and members in each work unit. This includes active outreach to reduce isolation and recidivism.
- The clubhouse evidences a commitment to securing and developing a range of choices of safe, decent, and affordable housing for all members.
- T.E. members report that housing, health and other needs are met.

# References

Beard, J.H., Propst, R.N.& Malamud, T.J. (1982). The Fountain House model of rehabilitation. *Psychosocial Rehabilitation Journal, 5(2)*, 47-53.

Bilby, R. (1992). A Response to the Criticisms of Transitional Employment. *Psychosocial Rehabilitation Journal, 16 (2)*; 69-82.

Bond, B., & Boyer, S. (1988). The evaluation of vocational programs for the mentally ill: A review. In J.A. Ciardiello & M.D. Bell (eds), *Vocational Rehabilitation of Persons with Prolonged Mental Illness.* (231-263). Batimore: Johns Hopkings University Press.

Bond, G. (1992). Vocational rehabilitation. In R.P. Liberman (ed.), *Handbook of Psychiatric Rehabilitation.* MacMillan; 244-272.

Dincin, J. (1975). Psychiatric rehabilitation (Reprinted). *Schizophrenia Bulletin, 13*; 131-137.

Glickman, M. (1992) What If nobody wants to make lunch? Bottom line responsibility in the clubhouse. *Psychosocial Rehabilitation Journal, 16(2)*; 55-59.

Kirszner, M.L., Baron, M.C., & Donegan, K. (1994). *Employer participation in employment programs for persons with long-term mental illness: A three year research study of employer involvement in transitional and supported employment.* Philadelphia: Matrix Research Institute.

Macias, C., Kinney, R., & Rodican, C., (1995). Transitional employment: An evaluative description of Fountain House practice. *Journal of Vocational Rehabilitation, 5*; 151-157.

Malamud, T. (1985), *Evaluation of Clubhouse Model-Community Based Psychiatric Rehabilitation,* National Institute of Handicapped Research. Contract # 300-84-0124.

Malamud, T.J., & McCrory, D.J. (1988). Transitional employment and psychosocial rehabilitation of individuals with prolonged mental illness. In J.A. Ciardello & M.D. Bell (eds), *Vocational Rehabilitaiton of Persons with Prolonged Psychiatric Disorders.* Baltimore: Paul H. Brooks. pp. 139-153.

Marrone, J., (1993). Creating positive vocational outcomes for people with severe mental illness. *Psychosocial Rehabilitation Journal, 17(2)*; 43-61.

Noble, J., (1991). *The Benefits and Costs of Supported Employment for People With Mental Illness and With Traumatic Brain Injury in New York State.* Research Foundation of the State University of New York. Final Report # C-00231801.

Phillips, J., & Biller, E., (1993). Transitional Employment Program for Persons With Long-Term Mental Illness: A Review. *Psychosocial Rehabilitation Journal, 17(2)*; 101-106.

Propst, R., (1992). Standards for clubhouse programs: Why and how they were developed. *Psychosocial Rehabilitation Journal, 16(2)*; 25-30.

Rubin, M. (1994). Andrew and fellowship: Response to disaster in a psychosocial rehabilitation program: A hurricane tolerance test of structure, philosophy, and methodology. *An Introduction to Psychiatric Rehabilitation,* IAPSRS. 281-293.

Ruffner, R. (1982). *Jobs are Important.* Washington, DC: Government Printing Office.

Rutman, I.D., & Armstrong, K. (1985). *A comprehensive national evaluation of transitional employment programs for the psychiatrically disabled.* (Unpublished paper). Philadelphia, PA: Matrix Research Institute.

*Transitional Employment,* A video training tape in the series, *Approaches in Psychosocial Rehabilitation.* Produced in 1983 under grants from the U.S. Department of Education, and Gateposts Foundation.

Treuer, E. & Rubin, M., (1993). *Direct Services Guide,* Fellowship House, Miami, Fl.

Vorspan, R. (1992). Why work works. *Psychosocial Rehabilitation Journal, 16(2)*, 49-54.

Waters, B., (1992). The work unit: The heart of the clubhouse. *Psychosocial Rehabilitation Journal, 16(2)*; 41-48.

Wehman, P., Kregel, J., & Shafer, M. (1989). *Emerging Trends in the National Supported Employment Initiative: A Preliminary Analysis of Twenty-Seven States.* Richmond, VA: Virginia Commonwealth University, Rehabilitation Research and Training Center on Supported Employment.

# Chapter 10

# Best Practices in Social Security Work Incentives

One of the biggest barriers to employment for persons with serious mental illness is the fear of losing medical and financial benefits provided by state and Federal agencies, most notably, the Social Security Administration (SSA) and the Health Care Financing Administration (HCFA). While the former provides cash benefits, in the form of Supplemental Security Income (SSI) and Social Security Disability Insurance (SSDI), the latter provides subsidized medical care to individuals eligible for SSA benefits in the form of Medicare and Medicaid, or other state-subsidized health care (e.g., AHCCCS in Arizona). For individuals experiencing serious mental illness and requiring access to primary health care and medication, the potential loss of these combined benefits represents a very real concern that should not and can not be overlooked when providing vocational rehabilitation services. For many people, and especially those with psychiatric disabilities, the process of applying for and being determined eligible for Social Security benefits is a very frustrating experience during which people are often forced to survive in abject poverty. As a result of this experience, an overall lack of information and understanding on the work incentive programs, and discouragement from others, many people choose not to work or work well below their potential in order to maintain their benefits and related health care coverage.

Work incentives were first introduced in 1972 with the Amendments to the Social Security Act. Since that time, the work incentive regulations have changed but the basic programs for both SSI and SSDI work incentives have remained consistent. Since Social Security benefits were not intended to be used as exclusive or permanent sources of income for people with disabilities, the work incentives are intended to give beneficiaries the support they need to move from benefit dependency to self-sufficiency (SSA Pub. NO. 64-030).

The Plan for Achieving Self-Support (PASS) and Impairment Related Work Expense (IRWE) are the work incentives with which rehabilitation professionals are most familiar. The PASS allows a person with a disability, who is either receiving or could be eligible to receive SSI, to set aside income and/or resources (i.e., wages, gifts, savings or other assets) for a specified period of time for a work goal (SSA Pub. NO. 64-030). The foundation of the PASS rests on the belief that it is a cost savings if SSA invests more money in a person for a short time in the form of SSI checks until he/she realizes gainful employment, versus paying that individual SSI or SSDI for their lifetime. Transportation is one of the most significant barriers people with psychiatric and other types of disabilities experience in finding and maintaining employment. As such, this is a necessary expense for which a PASS could be developed to compensate. PASS expenses are unique and so transportation could mean a bicycle, a car, taxi fare, a driver, plus any necessary operating expenses, or a number of other forms that would satisfy the need and allow for employment. There are several publications (Jones, 1995, APSE, O'Mara, 1995) available that explain the necessary planning activities required to develop a PASS.

Impairment Related Work Expense(s) (IRWEs) are the costs of certain impairment-related items and services that a person must purchase in order to work. The costs of approved IRWE(s) are deducted from the person's gross earnings in order to reduce the countable income and either increase the amount of their SSI check or continue their eligibility to receive SSDI.

IRWEs are allowable when the expense is related both to a person's disability and their work activity. Medication, therapy, or special training, which were paid for by the claimant, would be excludable expenses. Frequently, individuals report IRWEs such as job coaching, transportation, or medication to the SSA after the completion of a PASS. While the PASS and IRWE work very differently, both programs encourage and support people with disabilities in their work efforts by allowing them to collect higher benefit checks while working and/or extend the period that they are eligible to receive Social Security benefits while they are pursuing work activity.

Maintaining access to health care is of highest concern for many people with psychiatric disabilities. Employer-provided health plans are frequently not offered to people who work less than full time or within entry-level positions. Continued Medicaid Eligibility, also called Section 1619, is a work incentive which allows continued Medicaid coverage for SSI recipients whose earnings are too high to allow for an SSI cash payment. A similar work incentive is available for SSDI beneficiaries. The Continuation of Medicare Coverage provides at least 39 months of hospital and medical insurance to SSDI beneficiaries who continue to earn above $500.00 of gross monthly income after completing a trial work period.

The work incentive programs, including the PASS, IRWE, and continued health care coverage, are discussed comprehensively in the Red Book on Work Incentives (SSA Pub. NO. 64-030) which is available at most Social Security field offices.

The work incentive programs provide financial motivation and support for people as well as hope for their ability to access or return to employment. Until fairly recently, these programs were very under-utilized and claimants themselves were generally the least familiar with the opportunities available to them. This has begun to change over the last two to three years. During a one-year period, October 1991 through September 1992, the SSA reported a 69% increase in PASS utilization. As of September 1992, 5,280 SSI recipients nationwide were using a PASS to exclude earned and unearned income. While this number may appear impressive, it represented only 1.1% of the approximately 214,000 people who were working while receiving SSI payments due to a disability (SSA 1992, Table 13).

## Best Practice Indicators

Recently, the Community Rehabilitation Division, in conjunction with representatives of state and community behavioral health and vocational rehabilitation agencies, along with Social Security Administration representatives, established quality standards for providing and evaluating PASS services. These standards can be used by consumers, family members, rehabilitation counselors, case managers, and others to evaluate and guide the development and implementation of a PASS.

PASS Quality Standards and Procedures

CONSULTATION:

1. An initial *gratis* consultation should be provided to potential customers of PASS/IRWE services

2. The initial consultation period should be used to determine eligibility for using work incentives (SSI, SSDI, vocational goal, personal assets, work history, etc.) as well as current status with other support systems (i.e., BHS, VR, DDD, etc.). At this time, the customer's monthly expenses should be reviewed to ensure that they can afford to set aside income for PASS-related expenses.

3. Upon determining eligibility for a PASS, the PASS/IRWE Developer should explain PASS services, coordination with other agencies, Social Security requirements, fees for PASS services, and follow-up services (amendments, management, support). The PASS/IRWE Developer should provide the customer requesting services and/or designated representative with a written copy of the above information for their review.

4. After being provided with complete information on PASS Services, estimated income, and the obligations and responsibilities of PASS-recipients, the customer can choose to use the described services or pursue other similar services.

5. If the customer desires to use PASS Services, the PASS/IRWE Developer should have the customer and/or designated representative sign agreement forms for initiation of services (i.e. Consent to Release Information, Agreement to Pay, Management Agreement, etc.).

DEVELOPMENT:

1. The PASS/IRWE Developer, customer, and/or designated representative should schedule a follow-up session to define the goals of the PASS being developed, including: occupational objective, job market/employment potential, necessary expenses, length of time in accomplishing goal, accommodations, or other related planning topics.

2. VR counselors are not required to support the occupational objective identified PASS developed prior to initiation of VR services. If the customer is considering applying for VR services, it may be beneficial for him/her to delay PASS/IRWE submission until he/she is receiving VR services. The PASS/IRWE Developer should work collaboratively with VR counselors in the planning and development of the PASS and the vocational goal.

3. Professional vocational services from a Certified Rehabilitation Counselor, a vocational provider, or other vocational specialist should be used during the development and planning stages of the occupational objective.

4. The PASS/IRWE Developer should contact all other relevant support persons or systems prior to development of the PASS. The PASS/IRWE Developer should also coordinate the PASS occupational objective with the customer's IWRP.

5. The PASS/IRWE Developer should document all time spent with the customer or on their behalf and

should also make note of activities or objectives related to the time recorded.

6. PASS/IRWE Developer should explain **and** provide in writing, to the customer and/or designated representative, the customer's responsibilities in developing and managing his/her PASS. This must include a clear explanation of the possible ramifications of PASS money mismanagement and non-compliance.

7. For continued PASS development, the PASS/IRWE Developer should assign the customer follow-up tasks (i.e. expense estimates, loan rates, and applications, degree requirements or curricula, VR application, and any other relevant information or activities) to complete and also any needed guidance or support.

8. The PASS/IRWE Developer should prepare and provide a one-month individualized and detailed financial portrait for the customer showing the total amount of monthly income, earned and unearned, the amount to be sheltered by a PASS, and the amount to be allocated towards living expenses. This last figure needs to be more than or equal to the customer's current monthly budget.

9. The PASS/IRWE Developer should assist the customer in identifying a reliable individual to serve as a PASS Manager, upon approval of the PASS. This person should be available to work with the customer on an ongoing basis to assist in PASS implementation, accounting, amending, and compliance reviews.

10. The PASS should include the names, addresses and phone numbers of the customer, the PASS/IRWE Developer, as well as for the person/organization that will be managing the PASS.

11. In addition to the customer's and/or designated representative signature(s), the completed PASS should include the signature of the Vocational Counselor or other vocational specialist involved in the planning and development of the occupational objective.

MANAGEMENT:

1. The PASS/IRWE Developer should meet with the customer and/or designated representative immediately upon PASS approval to ensure proper account arrangements, customer understanding of money flow and their responsibilities with the PASS.

2. For a minimum of three months, the PASS/IRWE Developer or PASS Manager should meet with the customer and/or designated representative monthly to follow along on financial allocations and progress towards the approved occupational objective (i.e. academic enrollment and grade verifications, loan applications, proof of service/goods delivery for small businesses, applications for employment, employer performance reviews, and any other supporting materials).

3. The PASS Manager should notify SSA whenever they are aware that a customer is not complying with the PASS as approved. The customer and/or designated representative should be informed that this notification of SSA will occur before services are rendered and again at the time this action becomes necessary.

4. During PASS Management sessions, the PASS/IRWE Developer and the customer should calculate the total of receipts collected and the account balance and compare to accumulated sheltered amount to verify financial compliance. The customer should be provided with a written copy of all accounting and management services rendered by the PASS/IRWE Developer.

5. After at least three PASS Management sessions and *demonstrated compliance*, the PASS/IRWE Developer or PASS Manager should schedule quarterly or bi-annual, as appropriate, meetings with the customer and/or designated representative to total receipts and account balances. This should continue for the life of the PASS. Again, the customer should be provided with a written copy of all accounting/management procedures for their records.

6. The PASS/IRWE Developer or PASS Manager should accompany the customer and/or designated representative to SSA for scheduled compliance reviews and to discuss progress towards the approved occupational objective.

PASS NON-COMPLIANCE:

1. Upon awareness of non-compliance, the PASS/IRWE Developer or PASS Manager must notify SSA and the customer and/or designated representative.

2. The PASS/IRWE Developer or PASS Manager should schedule an immediate Compliance Review with SSA and the customer and/or designated representative. (This will determine the possibility of getting the PASS back into compliance.)

3. Should the PASS be continued, the PASS/IRWE Developer or PASS Manager should reinstate monthly PASS Management sessions to closely evaluate compliance. These sessions should be continued until the next scheduled Compliance Review with SSA.

4. The customer's PASS should be reviewed by the customer and the PASS/IRWE Developer or PASS Manager to ensure financial feasibility and the possible need for amending the Plan to encourage compliance.

5. Should the PASS be discontinued by SSA, all PASS Management services should be considered terminated and no further time should be billed to the customer.

6. Should the customer choose to pursue another occupational objective and a new PASS, the PASS/IRWE Developer should reinitiate the full process to providing PASS Development and Management Services.

7. The PASS/IRWE Developer should schedule a meeting with SSA, the customer and/or designated representative to discuss the outcome of the

previous PASS and the opportunity for a second PASS.

8. The PASS/IRWE Developer should collaborate with the customer and/or designated representative to work through problems and issues encountered during previous PASS to plan strategies to avoid similar situations.

The standards above emphasize a number of crucial elements that should be in place in any well written and managed work incentive plan. When assisting persons with serious mental illness, it is particularly important to address four primary issues. These include:

- consumer education
- proactive benefits monitoring
- realistic assessment of potential and appropriateness of the vocational goal
- provision of ongoing support

## Consumer Education

Frequently, claimants and their family members are poorly informed about their benefits, or reticent to do anything that may affect their benefits. As a result, individuals may be resistant to employment considerations, fearing loss or reduction of their benefits or may attempt to jeopardize rehabilitation and placement efforts. As such, it is critical that consumers and family members be provided information, including printed material, individual consultation, and group informational sessions, that comprehensively reviews the relative impact that returning to work will have upon their Social Security and other benefits (e.g. food stamps, housing assistance, health care, etc.). In addition to the various pamphlets and brochures produced by the Social Security Administration, a number of newsletters (Managing Disability and Diversity, PASS/IRWE Update, Supported Employment Works!, P.A.S.S. Planning), videotapes (Graduating to Independence), and computer software programs (CareerCALC, Excel) are available to help inform and educate consumers and family members regarding work incentives.

A crucial element in the education of individuals using PASS and IRWEs should be a careful review of the financial and legal responsibilities that these plans encompass. In essence, a PASS or IRWE represents a legally-binding agreement between the claimant and the Social Security Administration in which the claimant agrees to apply a stated amount of their personal resources to specified PASS/IRWE expenses. Failure to adhere to the specifics of the PASS/IRWE, or failure to report changes surrounding the PASS/IRWE or work activity can result in negative results such as overpayment (i.e. claimant owes money to the SSA), findings of PASS non-compliance, and PASS termination. The Social Security Administration has directed the work incentives in a manner that appears to be flexible and responsive to fluid rehabilitation plans. It is critical; however, that the claimant and any agencies or individuals assisting the claimant, provide the SSA with accurate and complete information related to work activity or to the implementation or fulfillment of a PASS or IRWE.

## Proactive Benefit Monitoring

While a PASS, IRWE, and the other work incentive programs (e.g. Section 1619 Work Incentives) are very beneficial for people with disabilities that want to pursue their vocational goals, the importance of rigorous monitoring of benefits cannot be over-emphasized. Benefit monitoring is intended to avoid benefit overpayment or termination, as well as to

proactively utilize the work incentive options and is well-supported by many professionals that have extensive experience in this area (APSE, 1990; Walling, 1995). Hinsberg and Horn described the benefit monitoring process as a series of sequential steps that include:

- obtaining a current and accurate record of a person's benefit status
- forecasting the impact of future employment on benefits
- open communication of information with claimant, family, or representative payee
- accurate and timely reporting of work earnings

- continued benefit and employment monitoring
- thorough attention to problem resolution

*(Hinsberg & Horn, 1990, 125-27).*

## Realistic Assessment of Potential and Appropriateness of Vocational Goal

With the recent increase in the work incentives there may also come an increase in the misuse of these programs as work incentives are developed that are neither appropriate or beneficial for the claimant. Such is the case when PASSes are developed based on vocational goals that are not feasible or realistic for the claimant to achieve. The objective of the PASS, especially, is to provide resources for people to assist them in achieving self-supporting employment. Developing a PASS with a primary purpose of ensuring a claimant remains on their benefits indefinitely is an example of incorrect use of the program. As such, it is

critical that professionals realistically and thoroughly assess and evaluate the long-term potential of each client to be gainfully employed. Without a comprehensive investigation, it is easy to depict a rosier picture with the use of a PASS than is realistic or likely to be feasible (Arino, personal communication, 1995).

When this happens, it is the claimant that suffers the most significant loss, financially, and perhaps even more importantly, the loss of an opportunity and dream to succeed (Arino, personal communication, 1995).

## Provision of Ongoing Support

The importance of proactively monitoring benefits and changes in work activity has been discussed. While not a required component of a PASS, it is recognized that, frequently, claimants need assistance and support in the implementation of their PASS and/or IRWE in order to administer the sheltered funds and continue progress towards their stated objectives. The use of monitoring services/case management is an allowable expense that

falls within the Social Security regulations (SSA P.O.M.S., 1994). The necessary support and assistance in the development phase of the vocational goals and the PASS is well-recognized, but too often, once a client has received the SSA's approval of their PASS, follow-along or ongoing support is not available. This is often the most critical time to work closely with an individual (Arino, 1995).

## References

Arino, R. (1995). Technical Assistant, Social Security Administration Field Office. Personal communication, June 30.

Association for Persons in Supported Employment (1990). *Project WIN Manual*, Richmond, Virginia, LM Friday, 6/30/95.

Emmons, T. (1994). *DisAbility Works Newsletter*.

Hinsberg, J., & Horn, B. (1990). *Using Social Security Work Incentives* Training Manual, Northern Arizona University, Institute of Human Development, Flagstaff, Arizona.

Jones, R. (1995). *A Step-By-Step Guide to Writing a Plan for Achieving Self Support for Submission to the Social Security Administration*. unpublished.

Moore, S.C., & Powell, T.H. (1990). Benefits and benefits protection for persons with severe disabilities entering supported employment: A guide for vocational rehabilitation counselors. *Journal of Applied Rehabilitation Counseling, 21(4);* 31-35.

O'Mara, S. (1995). *Understanding Social Security Benefits Manual.* Richmond, VA: Employment Support Institute, Virginia Commonwealth University.

Prero, A.J., (1993). Shifting the cost of self-pay for SSI workers in supported employment. *Social Security Bulletin, 56(1);* 44-51.

Social Security Administration, Office of Supplemental Security Income (1992). *Quarterly Report on SSI Disabled Workers and Work Incentive Provisions,* September.

SSA P.O.M.S., 00870.000, *Plans for Achieving Self-Support for Blind and Disabled People,* December, 1994.

US Department of Health and Human Services, Social Security Administration, Office of Programs, SSA Publication No. 64-030, ICN 436900, August, 1994.

Walling, M.E. (1995) Executive Director, Service Enhancements, Inc. Personal communication, May 30.

# Chapter 11

# Best Practices for Enhancing Consumer and Family Involvement in the Vocational Rehabilitation Process

The active involvement of consumers and their family members has long been recognized as a key element in the rehabilitation process. This involvement has been extensively discussed in the professional literature (Hatfield, 1988; Howie the Harp, 1994; Spaniol, Zipple, & Fitzgerald, 1994; Wintersteen & Young, 1988) as well as legislatively mandated in the Vocational Rehabilitation Act of 1973, as amended, and the Mental Health Act of 1986, as amended. However, well-controlled research studies assessing consumer and family participation in the rehabilitation process is scarce (Lewis & Frey, 1988; Moxley & Freddolino, 1990).

During this time, there has been significant growth in organizations such as the National Alliance for the Mentally Ill (NAMI) and other advocacy and self-help groups. Levine & Spaniol (1985) assert that the rapid growth of NAMI and other organizations was a reaction to the widespread disappointment of consumers and family members in service quality, lack of involvement, and inability of professionals to provide practical information and help. Torrey (1995) reports that there are over 1,000 chapters affiliated with NAMI. The growth of these organizations was facilitated in part by a series of initiatives undertaken by the National Institutes of Mental Health (NIMH). While the formation of groups like NAMI have had major influences in systems advocacy, consumer and family involvement has also been advanced at the level of individual client services. Service planning processes, like the Individualized Written Rehabilitation Program (IWRP) and the Individual Support Plan

(ISP), are person-centered planning processes that assume the active, informed, and meaningful involvement of the client in all aspects of their rehabilitation/treatment.

Consumer involvement has also been advanced by the development of a number of self-help and peer-support models. The active engagement of the mental health consumer in the rehabilitation process, both as a recipient and a provider of services, has grown partly due to the recognition that they are "... experts in their own right, having been educated by the grim realities of mental illness first hand..." (Hatfield 1988, p.83). For example, the use of peer counseling as a formal component of supported education programs has been repeatedly described (Cook & Solomon, 1993; Unger, 1993; Wolf & DiPietro, 1992). Similarly, recent research and demonstration projects have studied the efficacy of consumer case managers (Stoneking, Greenfield, Sundby & Boltz, 1991). Reflecting this focus on peer and consumer supports, the National Institute on Disability and Rehabilitation Research recently released a request for proposals calling for the funding of a Rehabilitation Research and Training Center expressly focused on peer support models in the rehabilitation process.

The development of consumer-run businesses and entrepreneurial enterprises has been repeatedly suggested as an alternative to traditional job placement and an effective means for involving consumers in the rehabilitation process. A number of demonstration projects, such as the Cookie Place in Providence,

Rhode Island (Lefley, 1985) and the Wyman Way Co-Operative in New Hampshire (Torrey, 1995), have provided examples in which consumers have been provided financial, administrative/business, and other supports necessary to launch and maintain private businesses. These businesses have included coffee shops, bakeries, banks, computer repair, landscaping, and building rehabilitation, to name a few. While a variety of how-to-manuals are available to assist individuals and agencies begin consumer-run businesses, very little is available regarding the long-term financial viability of these initiatives. Marrone (1993) notes that most consumer-run businesses are heavily subsidized by rehabilitation or social service dollars and experience chronic difficulty in generating a profit.

In this chapter, we will review various barriers to consumer and family involvement in the vocational rehabilitation process and present different models that have appeared in the literature to optimize such involvement.

## The Vocational Rehabilitation Act Amendments of 1992 and Consumer Involvement in the Rehabilitation Process

The 1992 Amendments to the Vocational Rehabilitation Act of 1973 provide clear and consistent directives for enhancing the level and quality of consumer involvement in the vocational rehabilitation process. This involvement is strengthened both within the Individual Written Rehabilitation Plan (IWRP) as well as in the establishment of State Rehabilitation Councils.

These Amendments specify that the IWRP must include "a statement by the individual (consumer) in the individual's own words describing how he or she was informed about and involved in choosing among alternative goals, objectives, services, entities providing services, and methods used to provide or procure such services" (U.S. Department of Education, 1993). These requirements are critical in their emphasis upon *informed choice*, concluding that a critical aspect of the IWRP development process is that of educating consumers about various rehabilitation alternatives *and* having an array of rehabilitation alternatives available to make this choice meaningful.

The 1992 Amendments also required all states to establish State Rehabilitation Councils. These councils, similar to the Behavioral Health Planning Councils which all states are required to have in place, must include a majority of persons with disabilities, as well as family members and disability advocacy group representatives. The purpose of these Councils is to provide the state VR agency with advice on a variety of issues, including:

- eligibility (including order of selection)

- the extent, scope, and effectiveness of services provided
- functions performed by the state agency that affect the ability of individuals with disabilities in achieving rehabilitation goals and objectives

These councils are also charged with conducting, to the extent feasible, a review and analysis of the effectiveness and consumer satisfaction of services provided, purchased, or authorized by the state VR agency.

At the heart of these Amendments is the underlying purpose of the VR Act to "empower individuals with disabilities to maximize their employment, economic self-sufficiency, independence, and inclusion and integration in the community" (U.S. Department of Education, 1993). This purpose is achieved in part by "respect for individual dignity, personal responsibility, self-determination and pursuit of meaningful careers." Harp, (1994, p. 84) describes empowerment as a "buzzword" that is often misunderstood, but "basically means power — power to control one's own life and the conditions that affect that life, at least with as much power as most people have." Harp conceptualized empowerment as occurring on four levels within the rehabilitation process:

1. Freedom of choice regarding individual services
2. Significant role in operation and decision making structure of program

3. Participation in system planning, evaluation and decision making
4. Participation in civic issues on community, city, county, state, and federal levels

These Amendments and their mandates provide provocative challenges not only to the federal-state rehabilitation system, but to community mental health, community rehabilitation, and other affiliated agencies and programs. The challenge is clear: people with disabilities and their family members must be involved as equal partners at all aspects of the rehabilitation service process, from identifying and prioritizing systems needs, to evaluating systems and programs, to selecting service providers, and identifying, developing, and implementing individual rehabilitation goals.

## The Use of Consumers to Provide Services in the Vocational Rehabilitation Process

A number of researchers have explored the use of consumers as providers of rehabilitation and therapy services, including peer counseling, case management, peer advocacy, and job coaching. In this section, we will review some of these applications, followed by a discussion of issues and strategies that community agencies should consider when using consumers as providers.

Shepherd (1992) identifies two basic concepts in employing consumers; jobs that are created specifically for consumers, and recruitment of consumers for regular staff positions. In the first category are positions such as self-help specialists or peer counselors. Shepherd warns that care must be taken in the first category not to "token-ize" or "ghetto-ize" these positions by isolating the positions by job, location, or pay scale. In the second category, there is a risk of "token-izing" by hiring only for menial jobs and not providing opportunities for career growth. In contrast, Curtis (1993) breaks down consumer colleague opportunities into five categories:

1. volunteer positions
2. on-the-job-training
3. created positions
4. set-aside positions
5. competitive positions

Volunteer positions include not only direct service, but colleague roles of governance, policy making, public education, etc. Lovejoy & Reinhold (1993) and Harp (1994) describe the value of volunteering as a steppingstone to employment. Harp reports that most of the paid consumer staff in his self-help organization started as volunteers. It should be pointed out that volunteering is a common way in which non-disabled persons test out their job interests and gain valuable skills and experience, as well as a valued and normal adult productive role. However, care must be taken to make sure the volunteer experience is not exploiting, but rather a normalizing one that provides good training, supervision, and growth opportunities. Set-aside positions are differentiated from created positions in that these are positions that exist in the agency but are enhanced by hiring a person who has the sensitivity brought about by direct personal experience. Set-aside positions are usually advertised with a stated preference for past service recipients. Created positions are developed specifically for consumers. Curtis points out that these positions are usually the ones that cause the most confusion for both consumer and non-consumer staff as the least clarified and tend to involve the person in the dual role of consumer and staff member.

Moxley and Freddolino (1990) describe the Client Support and Representation model (CSR) to help mental health consumers become empowered in the service development and delivery process. This model is designed to be *client driven* rather than *done to the consumer* out of the patronizing attitude of acting in their best interest. The CSR model advocates extended weekly help for approximately six months. Advocates operated in a *consultative relationship* directly with each consumer. Consumers were given help in identifying their own needs, establishing their own goals, identifying existing problems or barriers to meeting those needs, and determining what was needed to obtain resolution to the identified problems or barriers. Consumers were able to call on CSR advocates when they wanted skill development, technical assistance, or representation to solve issues at the lowest level of advocate involvement possible. The CSR model differed from traditional agency client rights approaches in that it is not reactive and tied to legal action. It is a proactive, iterative, needs-assessment process that seeks to assist consumers to identify problems in daily living areas that may pose barriers to rehabilitation. Overall success rates in achieving consumer-driven goals that were mutually agreed upon between consumers and advocates was over 80%.

Paulson (1991) described a program at the University of Cincinnati School of Social Work that was funded by NIMH to develop a special track to train masters-level social workers to work with persons with major mental illness. Course work and field placements were developed to promote work in the public community support system. The U of C program took on a special mandate to recruit and train both family members and consumers. Although the program was only in its third year of operation, the author provided tentative observations about both the training and role of family and consumer professionals that are applicable to the utilization of peer staff in general. The practice of providing field placements required students to relive past experiences and successfully learn to control and channel their feelings as an important part of their professional learning. One useful suggestion that came out of this for primary consumers was to consider both their field work and their first job placement as Supported Employment experiences. Difficulties that needed to be dealt with tended to focus on the additional need for support and supervision for both family members and consumers to help them sort out their own agendas, past experiences, and mixed feelings about working in the system as professionals. This included learning how to modify old patterns of advocacy, appreciate and respect the diversity of experiences of persons with mental illness and the unique responses that these individuals and their families made to managing the illness, and how to identify oneself as both a consumer and a professional.

Paulson (1991) identified a number of unique strengths and contributions that consumers and family members bring to service provision. These included:

1. consumers were more likely to know what is helpful in crisis situations
2. consumers were able to help other consumers learn how to survive in economically tight situations
3. consumers were able to be more accurate and credible, rather than moralizing, in helping educate other consumers with regard to medication compliance
4. consumers were likely to be more skilled at helping identify personal signals and circumstances most likely to exacerbate symptoms
5. family members were effective in eliciting other family members to share feelings about the impact of illness on their family
6. family members demonstrated particular aptitude in psycho-educational tasks, advocacy, evaluating alternative service opportunities, and accessing resources
7. family members also worked well with consumers and families in recognizing and developing joint strategies to deal with prodromal (symptom onset) signs.

Paulson emphasizes the importance of allowing consumer and family professionals to develop the full range of professional roles rather than limiting them as specialists for certain tasks. The implications for training of family members and consumers with bachelor or para-professional credentials might dictate involvement in a more narrow specialization of tasks based on the strengths and limitations identified by Paulson.

Kinney (undated) describes a program that conceptualized and implemented a consumer provider development process that assisted consumers engage in a variety of positions along a continuum of agency involvement. First, consumers would begin by serving on an elected Consumer Advisory Council (CAC) that functioned to advocate for consumer determined "good services" and to eliminate or minimize consumer determined "bad services." The CAC was actively involved in service system monitoring, quality assurance audits, advocacy, program design, and evaluation. By participating on the CAC, consumers start to be able to separate their own issues from system issues and deal with the beginnings of the duality of roles of being a consumer provider. Consumers on the CAC who displayed aptitude and interest then moved into paid peer counselor/on-the-job-training positions where they received training and supervision to further explore whether a career as a service provider was appropriate for them. The third step described by Kinney was a consumer designated position. The final step for consumers was to compete for other non-consumer designated positions. Sherman & Porter (1991) describe a similar program in Denver that engaged consumers as case workers.

## Issues and Concerns for Using Consumer and Peer Staff

The literature is consistent in describing barriers, disincentives, and issues that agencies and programs must consider when attempting to establish consumer positions within their organizations (Kinney, undated; Shepherd, 1992). Among the more frequently-identified issues are:

1. Consumer staff benefits and compensation.
2. The dual role of consumers as both recipients and providers of service and the potential loss of a social support system as these individuals may no longer be able to fully affiliate with other consumers, but may not be accepted or able to socialize with the "professionals."
3. The stigma and lack of credibility that consumer-staff may encounter from other staff within the agency, staff of affiliated agencies, or from other consumers or family members.
4. Identifying and accessing appropriate, reasonable accommodations.
5. Establishing and maintaining boundaries between therapy and work.

The literature consistently reports stigma and prejudicial rejection by professional and non-consumer staff as a key detriment to development of consumer staff (Macauley 1993; Besio & Mahler 1993; Shepherd 1992; Curtis, 1993). The authors point out that this stigma may manifest itself in many forms, including:

1. Perceiving work difficulties as manifestations of symptom and diagnosis rather than normal work task and relationship issues.
2. Exclusion of consumer staff from informal networks.
3. "Scapegoating" consumer staff by projecting organizational issues such as supervision and training, communication,

burn-out, etc., as consumer competency issues.
4. Hostility to reasonable accommodations as unfair or preferential treatment.

Curtis (1993), Shepherd (1992), and Wilson, et al. (1987), point out that the solutions to these issues require a long-term organizational commitment to ongoing staff training and education, and an examination and modification of agency policies and procedures. Staff education should include: sensitivity training to consumer issues; identifying and addressing organizational policies and practices which are barriers; involvement of staff in the design and implementation of the consumer colleague program to promote ownership of the program; and providing ongoing training that is relevant to tasks and always includes consumers and consumer viewpoints. Similarly, agencies implementing consumer staffing patterns should re-examine their agencies commitment to "reasonable accommodations," especially those policies affecting employee leave, access to fringe benefits, and job design/re-design. Finally, agencies must guard against "token-ism" or "ghetto-ism" in the development of consumer staff positions (Broadhurst 1993; Klossner & McDowell 1993). Developing career paths, continuums for consumer involvement (as previously described), and a meaningful commitment to the concept of reasonable accommodations are critical to ensuring that consumers are involved and provided the opportunities to become involved in meaningful and productive roles throughout the agency.

> ... former mental patients/mental health consumers have a unique contribution to make to the improvement of the quality of mental health services in many arenas of the service delivery system. The significance of their unique contributions stems from expertise they

have gained as recipients of mental health services, in addition to whatever formal education and credentials they may have. Their contribution should be valued and sought in areas of program development, policy formation, program evaluation, quality assurance, system designs, education of mental health service providers, and the provision of direct services (as employees of the provider system). Therefore, expatients/consumers should be included in meaningful numbers in all of these activities.

*(National Association of State Mental Health*
*Program Directors, 1989)*

## Establishing and Supporting Consumer-Run Businesses

One resource that has been largely overlooked by state rehabilitation agencies is the potential for developing supported employment placements in consumer-run businesses. As commented earlier by Howie The Harp, there is value in volunteering with peers as part of a legitimate vocational rehabilitation process. As consumer time in volunteering becomes more consistent consumer businesses often hire volunteers. State rehabilitation agencies can simultaneously support clients and develop client-run businesses by providing supported employment opportunities at these businesses. Some early consumer-run businesses were developed under the program philosophy known as the "Fairweather Lodge Concept" which was promoted by George Fairweather starting in the late 1960s. The Lodge Concept utilized professionals as consultants to help consumers establish cooperative living and business arrangements for its participants. Onaga (1994) reports that there are currently approximately 100 Lodges operating in the United States. More recent consumer-run businesses operate exclusive of professional assistance, and when they utilize any professional consultation it is usually after initial establishment of the project in response to a specific agreed-upon need rather than utilizing professionals as consultants to help establish the program as in Lodge programs.

Matrix Research Institute (1993) developed a program assessment tool, *Quality Indicators for Programs Operated by Persons with Disabilities.* It provides quality indicators for programs operated by persons with disabilities and could be a good starting point for consumer-run organizations to evaluate and market themselves. The quality indicators are organized into four categories:

1. *Values:* the program articulates and implements a set of fundamental beliefs about the value of persons with disabilities supporting their peers.

2. *Program Elements:* the program provides a wide range of supports, providing innovative, comprehensive, and measurably effective support services.

3. *Program Administration:* the program is well administered, with appropriate staffing, resources, and leadership.

4. *Dissemination:* the program has an interest in and capacity to serve as a model and resource for others developing programs operated by persons with disabilities, and is willing to offer others consultation, training, and technical assistance.

With the large number of consumer-run programs currently operating and being developed nationally, this assessment tool offers a useful framework of quality indicators for both self evaluation and for use by persons seeking to establish programs. To obtain a copy, write or call:

Matrix Research Institute
6008 Wayne Avenue
Philadelphia, PA 19144
Phone: (215) 438-8200
FAX :(215) 438-8337

# Enhancing Family Involvement in the Rehabilitation Process

The importance of including the family as partners in the vocational rehabilitation process becomes evident from the statistics showing that families are primary caregivers for many adults with serious mental illness. Spaniol, et al.(1994), observed that of 800,000 severely disabled ex-patients living in the community, 500,000 live with families. However, these families report infrequent contact with mental health and rehabilitation professionals, an average of less than once per month. Sixty percent of those surveyed by Spaniol expressed a need for more frequent and meaningful contact with the professionals involved in the treatment and rehabilitation of their family member. Lamb & Oliphant (1979) reported that 50-60% of all patients discharged from psychiatric hospitals return home; and Lefley (1987) estimates that up to 90% remain in contact with their families. Unfortunately, a review of the literature leads to the conclusion that the role of the family in the vocational rehabilitation of persons with serious mental illness has not been well focused either by empirical or descriptive studies.

Hatfield, et al. (1982), studied family caregivers of persons with mental illness to determine their needs, expectations of family therapy, and perceptions of how well their needs were met. The conclusion was that there was little congruence between families' expectations for services and the actual services they received. The majority of families reported seeking help in the practical management and rehabilitation of the relative with a mental illness, rather than assistance in family dynamics and behavior. Negative reports by families abounded as professionals were seen as often unable or unwilling to provide a clear diagnosis, basic information about the illness, practical advice about its management, community resources, or even information about the service system as a whole, and their own service agency in particular. Family members reported that services were often inadequately monitored or supervised. Hatfield goes on to point out a need for greater efforts to establish collaborative relationships between professionals and family members. Four primary obstacles to collaboration were identified:

1. *Difficulty in breaking down traditional hierarchical roles that separate professionals from non-professionals in Western society.* It is too easy for professionals to take on an authoritative stance, and families in turn take on the role of patient or client waiting to be directed or advised by the person in power.

2. *Confidentiality laws that complicate the process of collaboration.* Sometimes confidentiality is used as an excuse by professionals rather than finding ways to skillfully persuade clients that it is in their best interest to encourage the support of their families.

3. *Lack of understanding of the process of separation between client and family*, and lack of resources and skill in making that transition a smooth one.

4. Providers are often not prepared to handle the *normal and inevitable conflicts that arise when they collaborate with families*. It is important that in the collaborative model there is no right or wrong; there should be no winners or losers, but all must go away feeling that a win-win situation has been achieved.

While family members frequently report barriers and difficulties in accessing services, it is also important to note that the behavior, misconceptions, and desires of the family members may frequently present barriers to the rehabilitation process. These barriers can surface in a variety of contexts, as family members may perceive their member as incapable of employment or rehabilitation, may be un/mis-informed about the effects of paid employment upon Social Security benefits, may be concerned about the effect of any alteration in programming upon symptoms, or simply wish to maintain their family member in a stable and protective environment. While professionals may not always understand or agree with these and other family issues that may detract from the rehabilitation process, professionals must learn to accept these concerns as very real and very legitimate issues. As family members identify concerns regarding rehabilitation, professionals should be prepared to provide concise, factual information that allows family members to become more informed and educated about their concerns.

Community rehabilitation programs and rehabilitation professionals should find ways to collaborate with NAMI chapters and other family support groups, as they represent a vast resource of information, support, and assistance. Agencies can provide office and meeting space and encourage families and professional staff to join and participate in education and support activities. It should be considered a "best practice" for rehabilitation professionals to form close alliances so that clients, families and professionals can benefit. Hatfield (1988, p. 85) defines collaboration as "a relationship between families and providers which is based on a sense of equality, in which decisions are arrived at jointly, and in which responsibility for the outcome of the decisions is shared." The act of collaboration assumes that each of those involved has an area of expertise to contribute and that decisions made without including all affected parties are inherently unstable. The act of collaboration also assumes that stress and burnout is lessened when burdens and responsibilities are shared. This is just as true of professionals as it is of clients and families. Noble (1991) notes that collaboration should be *proactive and preventive*: "More attention should be paid to family needs before difficulties arise in the consumer's behavior or productivity on the job. In line with our interpretation of the meaning of the negative relationship between gross earnings and high levels of family counseling, here an ounce of prevention may well be worth a pound of cure. Apparently, once things begin to sour, scrambling to save a placement by increasing the number of family contacts and conferences with colleagues and other professionals does not work" (p. 26).

# References

Bergin, A., & Strupp, H. (1972). *Changing Factors in the Science of Psychotherapy*. New York: Atherton.

Besio, S.W., & Mahler, J. (1993). Benefits and challenges of using consumer staff in supported housing services. *Hospital and Community Psychiatry, 44(5)*; 490-491.

Birchwood, M., & Smith, J. (1990). Relatives and patients as partners in the management of schizophrenia. *Psychosocial Rehabilitation Journal, 13(3)*; 27-30.

Broadhurst, S. (1993). Co-optation: It's all too common. *Resources, 5(1)*; 16-17.

Chamberlin, J., Rogers, J.A., & Sneed, C.S. (1989). Consumers, families, and community support systems. *Psychosocial Rehabilitation Journal, 12(3)*; 93-106.

Cook, J., & Solomon, M. (1993). The community scholars program: An outcome study of supported education for students with severe mental illness. *Psychosocial Rehabilitation Journal, 17(3)*, 83-98.

Curtis, L.C. (1993). *Consumers as colleagues: Partnership in the workforce*. CCC - Trinity College.

Graziano, A., & Fink, R. (1973). Second-order Effects in Mental Health Treatment. *Journal of Consulting and Clinical Psychology, 40*; 356-364.

Hatfield, A. (1988). The role of the family in the rehabilitation process. Presented at *Rehabilitation Support Services for Persons with Long-Term Mental Illness: Preparing for the Next Decade*. Mary Switzer Memorial Seminar, Washington D.C.

Hatfield, A.B., Fierstein, R., & Johnson, D.M. (1982). Meeting the needs of families of the psychiatrically disabled. *Psychosocial Rehabilitation Journal, 6(1)*; 27-39.

Howie The Harp (1994). Empowerment of mental health consumers in vocational rehabilitation. *Psychosocial Rehabilitation Journal, 17(3)*; 83-89.

Hyde, A.P., & Goldman, C.R. (1993). Common family issues that interfere with the treatment and rehabilitation of people with schizophrenia. *Psychosocial Rehabilitation Journal, 16(4)*; 63-74.

Kaufmann, C.L., Freund, P.D., & Wilson, J. (1989). Self Help in the Mental Health System: A model for consumer-provider collaboration. *Psychosocial Rehabilitation Journal, 13(1)*, 5-21.

Kinney, H. (undated). *Metamorphosis from consumer to provider in a rural setting*.

Klossner, N.L., & McDowell, P.E. (1993). Guidelines for avoiding co-optation of consumers/employees. *Resources. 5(1)*; 14.

Lamb, H.R., & Oliphant, E. (1979). Parents of schizophrenics: Advocates for the mentally ill. In L.I. Stein (ed.), *Community Support Systems for the Long-term Patient*. (New Directions for Mental

Health Services, No. 2, pp.85-92). San Francisco: Jossey-Bass.

Lefley, H.P. (1985). Families of the Mentally Ill in Cross-Cultural Perspective, *Psychosocial Rehabilitation Journal, 8(4)*; 57-75.

Lefley, H.P. (1987). Aging parents as caregivers of mentally ill adult children: An emerging social problem. *Hospital and Community Psychiatry, 38*: 1063-1069.

Levine, I.S., & Spaniol, L. (1985). The role of families of the severely mentally ill in the development of community support services. *Psychosocial Rehabilitation Journal, 8(4)*; 83-94.

Lewis, M.R., & Frey, N.C. (1988). Changing attitudes towards parents of the chronically mentally ill. *Psychosocial Rehabilitation Journal, 11(4)*; 21-31.

Lovejoy, S., & Reinhold, B. (1993). From surviving to thriving: Consumers in the workforce. *Resources, 5(1)*; 12-13.

Macauley, R. (1993). Professionals need training to accept expatients as colleagues. *Resources, 5(1)*; 18.

Marrone, J., (1993) Creating positive vocational outcomes for people with severe mental illness. *Psychosocial Rehabilitation Journal, 17(2)*, 43-61.

Matrix Research Institute (1993). *Quality Indicators for Programs Operated by Persons With Disabilities.*

Moxley, D.P., & Freddolino, P.P. (1990). A model of advocacy for promoting client self-determination in psychosocial rehabilitation. *Psychosocial Rehabilitation Journal, 14(2)*; 69-82.

Noble, J., (1991). The benefits and costs of supported employment for people with mental illness and with traumatic brain injury in New York state. *Research Foundation of the State University of New York. Final Report # C-00231801.*

Onaga, E.E. (1994). The Fairweather Lodge as a psychosocial program in the 1990s. *An Introduction to Psychiatric Rehabilitation.* IAPSRS. p. 206-214.

Paulson, R.I., (1991). Professional training for consumers and family members: One road to empowerment. *Psychosocial Rehabilitation Journal, 14 (3)*; 69-80.

Shepherd, L. (1992). *So you want to hire a consumer: Employing people with psychiatric disabilities as staff members in mental health agencies.* CCC- Trinity College of Vermont.

Sherman, P. & Porter, R. (1991). Consumers as case workers. *Hospital and Community Psychiatry, May.*

Smith, M.K., & Ford, J. (1986). Client involvement: Practical advice for professionals. *Psychosocial Rehabilitation Journal, 9(3)*; 25-34.

Solomon, P., & Marcenko, M.O. (1992). Families of adults with severe mental illness: Their satisfaction with inpatient and outpatient treatment. *Psychosocial Rehabilitation Journal, 16(1)*; 121-134.

Spaniol, L., Zipple, A., & Fitzgerald, S. (1994). How professionals can share power with families: Practical approaches to working with families of the mentally ill. In W. Anthony and L. Spaniol (eds), *Readings in Psychiatric Rehabilitation.*

Stoneking, B.C., Greenfield, T., Sundby, E., & Boltz, S. (1991). *Adding trained consumers to case management teams as service coordinators: Program development, research design, accommodations, and early outcomes.* Paper presented at the 119th Annual Meeting of the American Public Health Association, Atlanta, Georgia, November 10-14.

Torrey, F.E. (1995). *Surviving Schizophrenia.* Harper Perennial, 3rd Edition.

U.S. Department of Education (1993). *A Synopsis of the Rehabilitaiton Act Amendments of 1992.* Washington, DC: Rehabilitation Services Administration.

Unger, K.V. (1993). Creating supported education programs utilizing existing community resources. *Psychosocial Rehabilitation Journal, 17(1)*; 11-23.

Wilson, S.F, Blanch, A., & Quinn, K. (1987). *The Role of Expatients and Consumers in Human Resource Development for the 1990s.* Northeast Consortium for Human Resource Development.

Wintersteen, R.T., & Young, L. (1988). Effective professional collaboration with family support groups. *Psychosocial Rehabilitation Journal, 12(1)*; 19-31.

Wolf, J., & DiPietro, S. (1992). From patient to student: supported education programs in southwest Connecticut. *Psychosocial Rehabilitation Journal, 15(4)*; 61-67.

# Chapter 12

## Best Practices in Providing Vocational Rehabilitation Services to Special Populations

Providing vocational rehabilitation to persons with serious mental illness demands diversity and flexibility on the part of the rehabilitation provider. The population we refer to as seriously mentally ill is a very diverse and heterogeneous population. Providing effective vocational rehabilitation services to this diverse group of individuals requires the development of systems and personal competencies that are effective in understanding these differences and responding to them in a manner that promotes career growth and realization of vocational potential. In this chapter, we will review best practices in providing vocational rehabilitation services to three special populations of persons with serious mental illness: persons of ethnic and cultural minorities; persons residing in rural communities; and persons who are dually diagnosed with a serious mental illness and a substance abuse disorder.

## Best Practices for Serving Persons of Ethnic and Cultural Minority Backgrounds

Successful vocational rehabilitation services to persons with serious mental illness are maintained on the theory of cultural pluralism and diversity. The cultural diversity shortcomings of human service agencies, including vocational rehabilitation, have been widely reported and have resulted in the adoption of multi-cultural perspectives to the provision of services. A multi-cultural perspective is based on a conceptual framework that acknowledges both the complex diversity of a pluralistic society as well as provides linkages or "bridges" of common interest, values, or concern among culturally-diverse groups. Adopting a multi-cultural perspective requires a coordinated, comprehensive, and *committed* plan of action that integrates multi-culturalism into all levels and aspects of the agency. First, let's take a look at some statistics that provide convincing evidence why we need to adopt a multi-cultural perspective.

I relate these stories of a time long gone because they capture all too well some of the pain experienced by those of us who are called minorities in America; they reflect the subtle types of disempowerment strategies that when, employed over again, erode our sense of self-esteem and self-confidence. I believe the impact of these experiences is absorbed so deeply within our souls that they become a part of our ancestral memory. No doubt, we struggle against their internalization, as we have for many years. And we rise, as we must, against them. Nevertheless, the legacy of shame and self-blame associated with these experiences can be overwhelming and a source of discouragement. Thus, I do not find it hard to understand the struggles of many of our young, their anger and disengagement, in a society that at best expresses ambivalence about their value in society.

*(Taylor Spriggs, March 24, 1994; Matrix Research Institute)*

Adopting a multi-cultural perspective requires the vocational rehabilitation provider to first acknowledge and understand their own cultural identity and its impact upon their approach to therapy. While we acknowledge the individuality of the human species, and the diversity and heterogeneity within most classifications, there exists some common, frequently-identified differences in the values, conceptual orientations, and traditions between dominant Euro-Anglo culture and most other groups. Some of these differences include:

| EURO-ANGLO CULTURE | MINORITY CULTURE |
|---|---|
| Value on choice, individuality, self-assertion, and ego development. | Most Eastern cultures[*] emphasize interdependence, the greater value of the community over the individual, and the spiritual balance of all living things. |
| Competition and conflict | Cooperation and compliance |
| Emphasis on action and outcomes | Emphasis on collective goals and collective responsibility |
| Direct eye contact shows respect and assertion | Direct eye contact among Asians and Native Americans may suggest disrespect, poor manners, or aggression. |
| Self-disclosure, self-adulation, and other behaviors that bring attention to the individual is acceptable and valued | Self-disclosure and other behaviors that bring attention to the individual are not acceptable or tolerated |

[*] The term "Eastern cultures" refer to the constellation of Native American, Pacific Islander/Rim, and Hispanic cultures.

As this country continues to experience cultural diversification, it is essential that a comprehensive understanding of these cultural distinctions, and their influence on effective rehabilitation planning for individuals with long-term mental illness, be developed. The importance of cultural understanding in the provision of mental health and rehabilitative services has been well documented (Yamamoto, Silva, Justice, Chang, & Leong, 1993; Griffith & Baker, 1993; Thompson, Walker, & Silk-Walker, 1993; Martinez, 1993; Marshall, Johnson & Lonetree, 1993; Marshall, Martin, Thomason & Johnson, 1991). Some strategies and recommendations for implementing multi-cultural perspectives within community mental health and community rehabilitation are summarized below.

## Systems Strategies

Systematically, the fields of vocational rehabilitation and community mental health, including federal, state, and local officials, as well as consumers, and providers, a number of strategies have been recommended to enhance the multi-culturalism of mental health and rehabilitation services. Issues of language, religion, family structure, and cultural beliefs regarding illness, disability, and recovery require unique approaches to effectively address the mental health and rehabilitation needs of individuals of ethnically-diverse backgrounds (Russo, Amaro & Winter, 1987). Among the recommendations that have been poised to meet these needs, the following have been consistently identified in the literature:

1. Enhance recruitment and retention of bilingual and/or bicultural workers;
2. Actively engage paraprofessionals, especially consumers and family members, in the provision of services;
3. Enhance the role of the consumer in treatment planning decisions;
4. Enhance the training opportunities available to persons of culturally-diverse heritage to enter the fields of mental health, rehabilitation, and related disciplines;
5. Incorporate the use of culturally-traditional approaches to healing within treatment modalities;
6. Develop assessment processes which are culturally sensitive; and

7. The design and delivery of services must proceed in the emergence of models which are consistent with cultural customs and beliefs.

*(Western Interstate Commission on Higher Education, 1993)*

- Locate offices and sites of services in community-based settings that are acceptable and appropriate locations for minority members to be found; and
- Avoid providing value judgments or offering subjective judgments regarding client behavior.

## Service Strategies

A number of strategies may be identified for community agencies to enhance their multi-cultural perspective:

- Provide program literature and materials in alternative formats for non-English-speaking consumers;
- Ensure availability of staff capable of verbally communicating with consumers in their native language;
- Meaningfully integrate non-traditional treatment methods (faith healers, sweat lodges, medicine man, songs) with traditional and established rehabilitation and treatment protocols;
- Allow for, and actively solicit, family involvement and participation in rehabilitation planning and treatment efforts;

## Staff Strategies

Rehabilitation counselors, case managers, and other human service professionals can engage in a number of professional behaviors and continuing education activities to enhance their effectiveness when working with culturally diverse clients. Sue (1992) and others suggest that professionals working with culturally diverse population address their:

- attitudes and belief systems regarding culturally bound groups;
- knowledge about the language, customs, societal norms, and values of culturally distinct groups; and
- skill in prescribing and implementing interventions with culturally diverse groups.

Staff working with culturally diverse groups should access educational and informational opportunities that will enhance their capacity in each of these domains.

# Best Practices in Serving Persons in Rural Communities

In addition to addressing the needs of clients from diverse ethnic backgrounds, it is important that vocational rehabilitation services be provided in a manner that is effective for individuals residing in smaller, rural, and often isolated communities. The U.S. Census Bureau, Department of Commerce, defines rural as "living in the open countryside or in towns of less than 2,500 inhabitants that lay outside urbanized areas" (The Rural Exchange, 1994). It is estimated that rural America covers over 90% of the land mass and contains over 25% of the population of the United States (Larson, Beeson, Mohatt, 1993). Rural residents experience incidence and prevalence rates of mental illness, substance abuse, emotional disturbance, and developmental disability equal to or greater than their urban counterparts, and yet only 25% of the rural poor qualify for Medicaid compared to 43% of the poor

in inner cities (Special Committee on the Aging, U.S. Senate, 1988). Rural areas have a disproportionate number of poor, elderly, children and adolescents, minorities, and migrant workers, all of who are high risk for developing or having mental disorders. Sixty-one percent of these rural Americans live in designated psychiatric-shortage areas (Larson, Beeson, Mohatt, 1993). While the past decade has evidenced significant enhancements in the quality and accessibility of vocational rehabilitation services within urban and suburban communities, similar enhancements within rural communities have been few and far between (Offner, 1992). In fact, Mathsen and Page (1985), in remarks before the House Select Education Subcommittee on the 1986 re-authorization of the Rehabilitation Act, noted:

... there seem to be more doors for the disabled in rural areas and less keys than their urban counterparts. We need to find ways to more effectively share information currently being generated, particularly to those who live and labor in rural isolation.

*(Mathsen & Page, 1985)*

These remarks underscore many of the difficulties facing rehabilitation in these communities; while rural communities may reflect more community cohesion and more "ownership" of the population, there continues to be major difficulties encountered in accessing employment and other community opportunities for individuals with long-term mental illness. The reasons for these difficulties are multiple. Rojewski (1992) identified five basic problems confronting rural rehabilitation. First, *employment opportunities are significantly fewer* in rural communities, making the role of the rehabilitation counselor particularly difficult. All too often, counselors must pose a difficult option to potential clients: relocate to an urban community or receive no services. Such an option is difficult for most and unattainable for many. Second, *rural residents are twice as likely to live in poverty*, as compared to their urban counterparts. In fact, residents of America's rural communities experience the nation's highest rates of poverty, cutting across all other demographic variables (William T. Grant Foundation, 1988). Third, *limited community services* complicate the role of the rural rehabilitation counselor, who must often attempt to create "something out of nothing" and, all too often, resort to transferring clients to urban units. Fourth, the *geographic distance and isolation* which typifies rural communities significantly impacts the availability and nature of rehabilitation services. Not only does this isolation remove the client from the service, but also isolates the service providers, fragmenting services and resulting in miscommunication or, worse yet, no communication. Finally, a host of other barriers may be identified which affect rural rehabilitation services. These may include the lack of acceptance of "outsiders," unwillingness to access "welfare" services, and rejection of exemplary programs due to their urban basis. Additionally, as Larson, Beeson, and Mohatt point out, rural practitioners are more likely to have to provide more and varied services to their patients because other support services (e.g., vocational rehabilitation, public housing, public transportation,

etc.) are nonexistent in the area (Larson, Beeson, Mohatt, 1993). Collectively, these issues point to the need for a re-examination of social and rehabilitation service approaches to rural communities.

## Recommendations for Providing Services in Rural Areas

- Policies affecting rural mental health care should be flexible enough to allow implementation based on local needs, resources, and values.
- The mental health system must include the perspective of consumers and their families. Consumers and family members should participate on all advisory boards, and all boards and panels that make decisions, to help humanize and sensitize the mental health system.
- Consumer-run alternatives to traditional mental health services should be supported in terms of availability and cost effectiveness.
- Linking different services systems (i.e., mental health and extension offices) through networks would allow mental health professionals to bypass some of the rural mistrust of newcomers and the stigma associated with mental illness. This may also increase the likelihood that an individual living in a rural area will seek help.
- Placing a number of different providers in the same clinic — the one-stop shopping concept — can alleviate some rural access problems.
- The barriers between different service providers must come down. Providers must work together to develop an integrated treatment plan which would avoid duplication of services or interference with other treatment regimes.
- Educate other service systems to increase understanding of mental illness and support for improving access to needed resources.
- Increase the availability of support services for persons with mental illnesses living in rural areas (i.e., non-clinical services).
- Support the development of consumer and family groups, both of which can provide a unique perspective to mental illness as well as insights into coping mechanisms.
- Adopt an empowerment/rehabilitation model for service provision which stresses the need to prevent

relapse through education and promotes the
concepts of illness management and recovery.

## Rural Mental Health Myths

It is **not** true that rural areas are stable, low-
stress environments that change very slowly
and are largely unaffected by national and
international trends and events.

It is **not** true that a health care system design
that meets the needs of urban Americans will
also meet the needs of rural Americans.

It is **not** true that solving the problems of
financial accessibility to mental health care will
make mental health services available and
accessible to rural Americans.

It is **not** true that rural populations experience
fewer mental disorders than urban populations.

It is **not** true that standard mental health
treatment modalities are appropriate for rural
areas and can be supported in that
environment.

It is **not** true that systems of care (health,
mental health, substance abuse, aging,
developmental disabilities, etc.,) in rural areas
are well integrated and work effectively with
one another.

*(National Association for Rural Mental
Health, Where We Stand,
Health Care Reform, Rural Mental Health)*

# Best Practices for Individuals with Co-Existing Disorders

Individuals who experience a substance abuse disorder
(abuse or dependence) in addition to a serious mental
illness have been a group who has been largely
excluded from access to vocational rehabilitation
options. Exclusion from access can come at many
points in the referral and intake system — mental
health professionals are hesitant to refer dually
diagnosed individuals for vocational services,
rehabilitation professionals are hesitant to accept them
for services when referred or self-referred.

Drake (1995) points out that the presence of a co-
existing disorder should not rule out a person's access
to vocational rehabilitation services. He recommends
functional assessment of the substance use, and its
interaction with the mental disorder, to determine the
type of service to be provided. He then recommends
tying the type of vocational service to the level of
recovery and impact on functioning. For example, an
individual who is currently abusing substances and is
also experiencing significant interference from
symptoms of mental illness (possibly because of the
exacerbating effects of substance use) might be
considered for transient or short-term, flexible jobs

(e.g., inserting flyers into newspapers, putting flyers on
windshields, day labor). This meets the immediate need
and request of the person without excessive use of
supports and resources that might not be well used at
this point in recovery.

A person who is currently abusing substances and is
also making a significant effort toward abstinence and
sobriety might be considered for vocational
rehabilitation and supported employment in conjunction
with treatment for the co-existing disorder. Indeed,
Drake points out, admission into the vocational field
while still working on sobriety can be a much better
catalyst toward change than having to achieve sobriety
as a prerequisite to vocational rehabilitation entry.

A person who is currently maintaining sobriety and is
in vocational rehabilitation would require significant
support (off site) to maintain abstinence while
negotiating and coping with the many changes in their
life. An employment support group that is created for
persons with co-existing disorders and focuses on
sobriety issues while at work would be one ideal vehicle
for achieving this.

# References

Acosta, F.X. (1977). Ethnic variable in psychotherapy: The Mexican-American. In Martinez, J.L. (ed.) *Chicano Psychology*. New York: Academic Press.

Acosta, F.X. (1979). Barriers between mental health services and Mexican Americans: An examination of a paradox. *American Journal of Community Psychology, 7*: 503-520.

Bennet, J.O. (1985). The impact of race, socio-economic status and folk beliefs on the perception of mental illness. *Dissertation Abstracts International, 46(3-B)*; 951.

Drake, R. (1995). Substance abuse and mental illness: Recent research. *NAMI Advocate, Jan/Feb.*

Flores, P.J. (1986). Alcoholism treatment and the relationship of Native American cultural values to recovery. *International Journal of the Addictions, 20*: 1707-1726.

Foster, D.V. (1988). Consideration of treatment issues with American Indians detained in the Federal Bureau of Prisons. *Psychiatric Annals, 18*: 698-701.

Gaw, A. C. (1993). *Culture, Ethnicity, and Mental Illness.* American Psychiatric Press, Inc.

Goedde, R.C. (1993). Chronic and severely mentalli ill Chicanos, Cubans, and African Americans enrolled in a community mental health system: Ethnic community supports and help seeking behavior. *Dissertation Abstracts International, 53*: 5637-B--5638-B.

Griffith, E.H., & Baker, F.M. (1993). *Psychiatric Care of African Americans. Culture, Ethnicity, and Mental Illness.* American Psychiatric Press, Inc.

Hough R.L., Landsverk J.A., Karno M.,et al. (1987). Utilization of health and mental health services by Los Angeles Mexican Americans and non-Hispanic Whites. *Archives of General Psychiatry.* 44: 702-709.

Jones, E.E., & Korchin, S.J. (eds.) (1982). *Minority Mental Health.* New York: Praeger Publishers.

Jones, J.M. (1984). Black cultural perspectives. *Clinical Psychologist, 37(2)*; 58-62.

LaFramboise, T. (1990). Counseling intervention and American Indian tradition: An integrative approach. *Counseling Psychologist, 18*: 628-654.

Larson, M.L., Beeson, P.G., & Mohatt, D. (1993). *Taking Rural Into Account.* Center for Mental Health Services, p. 1-41. Report on the National Public Forum Co-Sponsored by the Center for Mental Health Services, Lincoln, NE: June 24.

Leung, P. (1988). Asian Americans and rehabilitation: Some important variables. *Journal of Applied Rehabilitation Counseling, 19(4)*; 16-20.

Liu, W.T. (1986). Culture and support. *Research and Aging, 8(1)*; 57-83.

Lowrey, L. (1983). Cultural diversity in management. *Journal of Rehabilitation Administration, 7(2)*; 45-51.

Marshall, C.A., Johnson S.R. & Lonetree, G.L. (1993). Acknowledging our diversity: Vocational rehabilitation and American Indians. *Journal of Vocational Rehabilitation, 3(1)*; 12-19.

Marshall, C.A., Martin, W., Thomason, T.& Johnson, M. (1991). Multiculturalism and rehabilitation counseling training: Recommendation for providing culturally appropriate counseling services to American Indians with disabilities. *Journal of Counseling and Development, 70(1)*; 225-234.

Martinez, C. (1993). Psychiatric care of Mexican Americans. In A.C. Gaw (ed.) *Culture, Ethnicity, and Mental Illness.* Washington, DC: American Psychiatric Press, Inc.

Medina, S., Marshall, C., & Fried, J. (1988). Serving the descendants of Aztlan: A rehabilitation counselor education challenge. *Journal of Applied Rehabilitation Counseling, 19(4)*; 40-44.

O'Connell, J.C. (ed.) (1987). *A study of the special problems and needs of American Indians with handicaps both on and off the reservation, 1.* Flagstaff: Northern Arizona University, American Indian Rehabilitation Research and Training Centers.

Offner, R. (1992). Disability and rural independent living: Setting an agenda for rural rehabilitation. *Human Services in the Rural Environment, 15(3)*; 6-8.

Rojewski, J.W. (1992). Vocational rehabilitation in rural America: Challenges and opportunities. *American Rehabilitation, 18(1)*; 39-44.

Russo, Amaro & Winter (1987). The use of inpatient mental health services by Hispanic women. *Psychology of Women Quarterly, 11(4)*; 427-41.

Scott, A. (1990). *Latino Mental Health: Implications for the Workforce.* Human Resources Association of the Northeast.

Scott, A. (1990). *Latino Mental Health: Implications for the Workforce*. Human Resources Association of the Northeast.

Sue, D.W. (1992). The challenge of multiculturalism: The road less traveled. *American Counselor, 1(1)*, 6-14.

Sue, S. (1991). Community mental health services for ethnic minority groups: A test of the cultural responsiveness hypothesis. *Journal of Consulting and Clinical Psychology, 59*: 533-540.

Thompson, J.W., Walker, R.D., Silk-Walker, P. (1993). Psychiatric care of American Indians and Alaska natives. In A.C. Gaw (ed.) *Culture, Ethnicity, and Mental Illness*. Washington, DC: American Psychiatric Press, Inc.

Trevino F.M., Bruhn, J.G., Bunce, H. (1979). Utilization of community mental health services in a Texas-Mexico border city. *Social Science Medicine, 13A*: 331-334.

Trevino, F.M., Rendon, M.I. (1994). *Mental Illness/Mental Health Issues, Latino Health in the US: A Growing Challenge*. Chapter 15: 447-475.

U.S. Senate, Special Committee on Aging (1988).

Wade, P. (1991). Culture sensitivity training and counselor's race: effects on black female client's perceptions and attrition. *Journal of Counseling Psychology, 38*: 9-15.

Western Interstate Commission for Higher Education (1987). *From Minority to Majority: Education and the Future of the Southwest*. Boulder: Western Interstate Commission for Higher Education.

Western Interstate Commission for Higher Education. (1993). *The Journey of Native American People with Serious Mental Illness*. (Summary of National Conference) Boulder: Western Interstate Commission for Higher Education.

What is Rural? (1994). *The Rural Exchange, 7(2 & 3)*; 5.

William T. Grant Foundation Commission on Work, Family, and Citizenship. (1988). *The forgotten half: Pathways to success for America's youth and young families*. Washington, DC: Author.

Yamamoto, J., Silva, J. A., Justice, L. R., Chang, C. Y. & Leong, G. B. (1993). *Cross- Cultural Psychotherapy. Culture, Ethnicity, and Mental Illness*.

# CAREER RECOVERY
## BEST PRACTICES IN THE VOCATIONAL REHABILITATION
## OF PERSONS WITH SERIOUS MENTAL ILLNESS

### Michael S. Shafer, Anne Middaugh, Marshall Rubin, and Rosemary Jones

A state-of-the-art resource on helping people with psychiatric disabilities obtain employment, this book comes at a time when people with mental illness are experiencing the highest unemployment rates of ANY group in the United States. This well-researched book covers in twelve chapters the best practices on various topics in vocational rehabilitation related to people with serious psychiatric disabilities. Topics include:

- ❖ consumer involvement
- ❖ interagency collaboration
- ❖ vocational assessment
- ❖ supported education
- ❖ supported employment
- ❖ transitional employment
- ❖ job development

*Career Recovery* will be a much-used resource for any vocational rehabilitation counselor, mental health professional, supported employment specialist, or any job seeker with a mental illness.

$29 ❖ ISBN 1-883302-24-2 ❖ 8.5" x 11" ❖ 109 pages

❖

ALSO FROM TRN...

# WORKING ON THE DREAM
## A GUIDE TO CAREER PLANNING AND JOB SUCCESS
### *A CAREER PLANNING TOOL FOR PERSONS WITH MENTAL ILLNESS*

### Written by Don Lavin and Andrea Everett; Edited and Produced by Beth DePoint

This hands-on manual was written to educate people with serious mental illness and the employment professionals who work with them. It promotes "person-centered" career development principles for rehabilitation. The book encourages readers to take charge in choosing a career path, developing job goals, and taking responsibility for planning their job search strategies. *Working on the Dream* includes a structured, self-administered career planning profile.

*Working on the Dream* is for job seekers with mental illness, rehabilitation counselors, employment professionals, psychiatrists, psychologists, and other mental health professionals.

$18.50 ❖ 8.5" x 11" ❖ 136 pages ❖ spiral bound

- - - - - - - - - - - - - - - - - - - - - - - - - - - - - - - - - - - - -

Return form to: TRN, Inc., PO Box 439, St. Augustine, FL 32085-0439 USA.
Please make checks payable to TRN, Inc. Our EIN is 59-3215621.
**All orders must include purchase order number or payment; or you can charge your order by phone.**

Name _____

Organization _____

Address _____

City _____

State/Province _____

Zip/Postal Code _____

Phone (_____) _____

E-Mail Address _____

☐ Please send me _____ copies of *Career Recovery* at $29.00 US each.

☐ Please send me _____ copies of *Working on the Dream* at $18.50 US each.

**SHIPPING WITHIN UNITED STATES**
$3 US for 1st book; $1 each additional book.
Contact us for shipping cost over 10 items or to other countries.

**Phone Orders: 904-823-9800 ❖ Fax Orders: 904-823-3554**
❖
Visit our Web site at http://www.oldcity.com/trn
or e-mail us at trninc@aol.com